Anthony

Enjoy t'

Martin

SECRET
SOUTHAMPTON

Martin Brisland

First published 2019

Amberley Publishing
The Hill, Stroud
Gloucestershire, GL5 4EP

www.amberley-books.com

Copyright © Martin Brisland, 2019

The right of Martin Brisland to be identified as the
Author of this work has been asserted in accordance
with the Copyrights, Designs and Patents Act 1988.

ISBN 978 1 4456 8555 7 (print)
ISBN 978 1 4456 8556 4 (ebook)

British Library Cataloguing in Publication Data.
A catalogue record for this book is available from the
British Library.

Origination by Amberley Publishing.
Printed in Great Britain.

Contents

Introduction

For many years the port of Southampton was known as the 'Gateway to the World', and is still the home of the merchant navy. However, it was once seen as a place to travel through, not to linger in. Badly damaged by Second World War bombing raids, much of the rebuilding of the 1950s and 1960s was getting rather jaded. Since we were elevated by the Queen from a town to a city in 1964, Southampton has continued to grow into the richly diverse, thriving city and port we see today. Nowadays it is a vibrant city undergoing major redevelopment and is increasingly seen as a destination in itself. A projected bid for City of Culture in 2025 is part of that process.

There have been a great many Southampton books written over the years – some full histories, some on certain suburbs, some on the docks or the *Titanic*, some on the trams that ended in 1949, some with old photographs, some on its role in the design and production of the Spitfire, and some on its pubs or Southampton Football Club. So, what makes this book on Southampton different? For some years I have worked as a tour guide with See Southampton. Their aim is to promote the city and its communities, culture and heritage. I have helped develop the See Southampton website, its Facebook and Twitter pages and met many local organisations and members of the public. Along the way I have picked up many weird, wonderful, strange but true facts and lesser-known stories that I would like to share with you. Hopefully this is a fun yet informative book that everyone can dip into and find something of interest. If you go away saying 'Well I never knew that' or 'I have always wondered what that meant' then my job is done. Southampton is a city to be proud of. I trust that *Secret Southampton* will help locals and visitors alike discover some of its hidden treasures.

1. Secret People

Harry Houdini and Billy Reid

On 29 April 1911, world-famous escapologist Harry Houdini (1874–1926) patented his famous Chinese Water Torture trick at the site of the former Hippodrome in Ogle Road, just off Above Bar. This theatre closed in 1939 and the site was bombed in the Second World War. Houdini's ankles were locked into stocks, which were then hoisted up. He was then lowered into a water-filled box that was padlocked shut. Suspended upside down underwater with his feet immobilised, Houdini had only minutes to hold his breath before he would drown. The audience for this, Houdini's most celebrated feat of escapology, numbered just one paying customer. The performance was an unadvertised matinée with the seats priced at a guinea. Its purpose was to copyright Houdini's latest act as a 'play' and safeguard it from imitators. The Hippodrome was the first 'public' performance he ever gave of this trick, though it has never been recognised by a plaque.

There is, however, a plaque to Billy Reid (1902–74), who was born in St Mary Street. A riveter at the docks, he soon began earning extra money as a musician. Billy played piano

Billy Reid was the first British songwriter to top the US charts three times, a feat not bettered until the Beatles came along.

while his brother George played saxophone. In the 1920s the brothers turned professional and left Southampton. Billy took up the accordion, the instrument for which he is best remembered. In the 1940s he wrote a number of successful chart hits for his partner Dorothy Squires. He also wrote songs recorded by Louis Armstrong, Ella Fitzgerald and Frank Sinatra. At one time he was reputed to be earning £1,000 a week and his best known hit was 'The Gypsy' from 1945. Billy was the first British songwriter to top the US charts three times, a feat not bettered until the Beatles came along. Unfortunately, he invested his money unwisely and became bankrupt in 1958. Billy later moved to the Isle of Wight, where he died aged seventy-one.

The Musical Verne Sisters
These sisters lived at No. 12 Portland Street, Southampton, from 1866 to 1892. Their parents, both music teachers, were Germans with the surname Wurm. They changed this to Verne when they moved to England.

Mathilde Verne (1865–1936) made her name as a piano teacher to many famous people, including Lady Elizabeth Bowes-Lyon, the later Queen Mother.

Alice Barbara (1868–1958) was a composer. Sir Malcolm Sargent conducted a performance of her most famous work, 'Mass' in B-flat.

Adela (1877–1952) was taught piano by the celebrated Ignace Jan Paderewski. She went on to be regarded as one of the greatest pianists of her era. She toured with great success in many parts of the world and was the first British artist to give a solo recital at the Albert Hall. Adela today has a close with her name in Southampton's Botley Road.

The highly musical Verne sisters lived at No. 12 Portland Street, Southampton, from 1866 to 1892.

Craig David

On the post-war Holyrood estate is Queens House. The estate was designed by Lyons Israel Ellis, who also designed Wyndham Court near the Southampton Central station. In 2012, seven tiled murals designed by Anna Vickers depicting scenes from Southampton's history were installed on the estate's blocks. The flats are heated with water from a local geothermal energy company.

It is here that singer and DJ Craig David (b. 1981) grew up and attended the nearby St Mary's C of E Junior School in Ascupart Street. He then attended Bellemoor School and Southampton City College before his rise to fame. David, an avid supporter of Southampton FC, performed a series of hometown gigs at the Mayflower Theatre in 2017.

DID YOU KNOW?
Some Southampton street names such as Ascupart Street, Bevois Valley and Josian Walk recall the popular medieval legend of Sir Bevois and Ascupart – a knight and his giant squire.

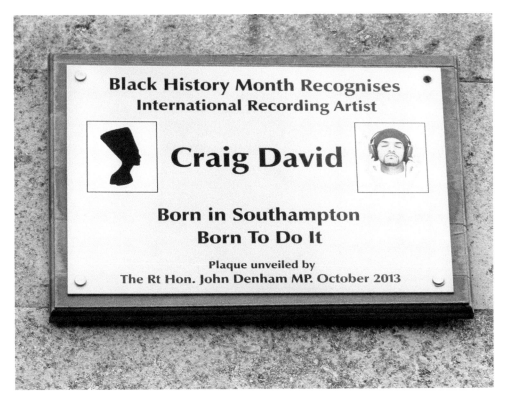

Craig David has had seven UK Top 40 albums and has sold 15 million copies worldwide.

Benny Hill (1924–91)

Alfred Hawthorne 'Benny' Hill was born in Southampton's Bernard Street. His father had been a circus clown and later managed a surgical appliance company. His grandfather used to take him to watch variety shows every Wednesday at local theatres in Southampton where young Alfred picked up the skills of timing and soon began to mimic the performers. Benny had great admiration for the violin-playing, straight-faced American comedian Jack Benny. He took his idol's surname as his forename for his stage act.

By 1955, 'Benny' Hill was on TV and by the mid-1970s his show had high viewing figures. He became a huge international star – perhaps because many of his routines were mainly visual and often based on old silent comedies. His self-composed song 'Ernie (The Fastest Milkman in the West)' reminds us of his early job as a milkman in neighbouring Eastleigh. It was the Christmas No. 1 in 1971. By the 1980s Thames Television decided that scantily clad girls, double entendres and slapping old bald men on the head was not in tune with the times. However, in the USA and elsewhere, such as Australia, audiences stayed loyal. In 1986, the inmates of a Californian prison threatened a riot when they heard that the evening's *Benny Hill Show* was not going to be shown.

Benny lived very simply in his Westrow Gardens house when in Southampton. I once stood next to him shopping with a string bag for fruit and veg at Delbridges in Bedford Place. He also liked to have a quiet half pint alone at the Royal Pier gatehouse.

Benny Hill is buried at Hollybrook Cemetery, near to Southampton General Hospital.

Benny died alone in his London flat watching TV, and his estimated £10 million estate was divided between nieces and nephews. Benny is buried at Hollybrook Cemetery, near to the General Hospital. There were incorrect rumours that he had asked that jewellery should be placed in his coffin and there was an attempt to break into his grave. Subsequently, his family arranged a thick, heavy stone to be placed horizontally over the grave.

There is a Benny Hill Close in Eastleigh, but no recognition of him in Southampton other than a small plaque in the grounds of the present Hill Lane site of his old school, Richard Taunton's Sixth Form College.

Rose Foster (1884–1959)

Rose was born at No. 7 Highcrown Street, and Highfield Church records say on 16 November 1884 baby Rose was received into the church's congregation. This may indicate she was not expected to live very long. Rose had a rare congenital condition of phocomelia, which was described as having limbs like a seal's flippers. In those times the only way she had of earning a decent living was to join the then popular travelling fairgrounds exhibiting 'freak and novelty shows'. Performing as 'Miss Rosina, The Eighth Wonder Of The World', the 26-inch-tall Rose toured the world, appeared before royalty and worked with Barnum and Bailey. When Rose retired she went to live with her sister in Belmont Road, Portswood. Today we have a more positive attitude to those with disabilities, as shown by the statue of Alison Lapper (b. 1965), who also has phocomelia, that was outside the National Gallery in Trafalgar Square and also featured in the 2012 Summer Paralympics opening ceremony.

Tommy Cooper (1921–84)

The comic magician often visited his mum at her shop at No. 124 Shirley Road, Southampton. It is a chippy today but back then she sold wool, costume jewellery and similar bits and bobs. He would take her for lunchtime meals to the Cowherds pub on the Avenue. He was not born in Southampton but spent some time locally in Langley on Waterside in his early years and was an apprentice at the British Powerboat Company in Hythe.

Muhammad Ali (1942–2016)

In October 1971 the most famous sporting superstar on the planet at the time was in a local supermarket in Hedge End, Southampton. The former world heavyweight boxing champion, Muhammad Ali, made an appearance at the then Fine Fare supermarket – today a Country Casuals store. Renowned for his 'Ali shuffle', he was the boxer who 'floated like a butterfly and stung like a bee'. Ali had been brought here by the makers of Ovaltine to promote their malted milk drink. He arrived in Southampton by train and was taken to the Fine Fare store where he autographed tins of Ovaltine. Later at the former Polygon Hotel, then the most prestigious in Southampton but since demolished to make way for flats, the boxer was surrounded by a media crew and fans. A family from Townhill Park in Southampton appeared by the side of the boxer. With his usual amicable 'tact' he said to a child, 'How come you are so pretty when your dad looks like that!' Ali

Left: Tommy Cooper's mother had a shop at No. 124 Shirley Road – a chippy today.

Below: In October 1971, Muhammad Ali was in a local supermarket in Hedge End.

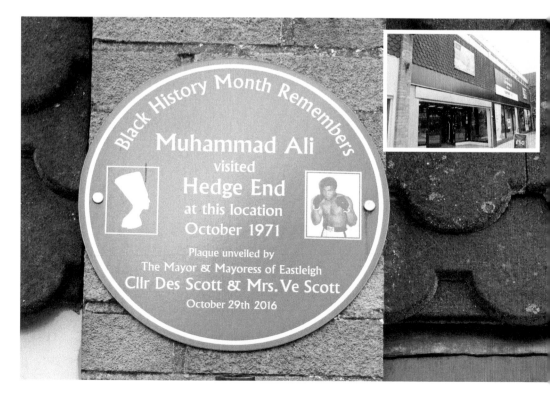

would not promote alcohol, cigarettes or beer. 'I have turned down offers of 10 million dollars to advertise things I do not believe in,' said Ali. He was stripped of his world title for refusing to do his army service in the United States during the Vietnam War. The visit is commemorated by a plaque organised by Black History Month.

Eric Meadus (1931–70)

Born in Rigby Road, Bevois Mount, Eric grew up on Lobelia Road, Bassett. The area near the University of Southampton is known locally as the Flower Roads, after the street names. Much of his output features the Bassett and Swaythling houses and open spaces from this home patch. Meadus showed an early aptitude for drawing and became an accomplished

An Eric Gill-designed mural above the former Bank of England building in the High Street.

draughtsman. His employers, Pirelli General, called on his talents as a cartoonist for their national house magazine, *Cable*. He died aged only thirty-nine, so his artistic span was brief. It is estimated he may have produced some 1,000 works, but destroyed many. The First Gallery in Bitterne owns a substantial number of Meadus's works and Southampton City Art Gallery holds some Eric Meadus drawings and paintings. In 2011, a small development of social housing next to Swaythling station was named Eric Meadus Close.

Eric Gill (1882–1940)

Eric Gill's mural is above the former Bank of England building in the High Street. It was later the Walkabout bar, after that Wahoo! and is currently vacant. Gill was once named Royal Designer for Industry, the highest British award for designers, by the Royal Society of Arts. He designed the figures of Ariel and Prospero (from *The Tempest*) at the BBC's Broadcasting House in London. However, his reputation today is sullied by some unpleasant revelations about his personal life.

Herbert Collins (1885–1975)

A plaque by Market Buildings in Swaythling reads: 'This place is dedicated to the memory of Herbert Collins. Architect and Worker for Peace.' Today his work is all around Southampton, but the man behind it is not well known. Former city architect Leon Berger said, 'He was certainly the most important architect in the housing field that Southampton has ever seen.' Collins moved from London in 1922 and became very interested in local affairs. He was involved with the construction of housing estates such as Uplands,

Collins's work is all around Southampton, but the man behind it is not well known.

Highfield; Swaythling Housing Society; Bassett Green; Thornhill Park; Orchards Way, West End; and Coxford. He designed flats including in Lodge Road, Canute Road and Henstead Road, Polygon. In 1930 he also designed Southcliff House in Southcliff Road, Inner Avenue, which contains six flats where the housing society's female rent collectors lived. He designed his own home in Brookvale Road and many other local projects – totalling around 1,500 premises. Many are simple two-storey houses in a simple Georgian cottage style, often set near a small green with tree bordered roads. Pevsner's *Buildings of Hampshire* (1967; revised 2018) said his Uplands estate was 'the best piece of suburbia in Southampton'. The leases do not allow for radical alterations, thus preserving their original identity.

A pacifist, in 1924 he founded the local branch of the League of Nations Union. Collins founded a charity shop (possibly the first in Southampton!) to raise funds. His offices were at No. 32 Carlton Crescent and he continued to work there up to his death in his ninety-first year. Collins is commemorated by a memorial gate in Highfield and a blue plaque on his home.

Ellis Martin (1881–1977)

A Collins-designed house in Highfield Close, Portswood was the home of Ellis Martin. He was an artist employed from 1919 to 1940 by the Ordnance Survey (OS) to illustrate the covers of their maps. These scenes helped OS maps to sell in large quantities. Ellis had attended the Slade School of Fine Art, where he was a contemporary of artist Augustus John who lived at Fordingbridge on the edge of the New Forest. OS maps with Ellis's distinctive illustrations are very collectible today.

DID YOU KNOW?
The 1810 OS map of Southampton still shows the town gallows, last used in 1785. They can be seen marked at the top of Southampton Common, close to Burgess Road. Just inside Ocean Village there was also an Admiralty gallows, today the site of a convenience store.

Ellen Wren (1845–94)

Today Simnel Street is a pleasant residential area, but it was once part of the overcrowded Victorian slums of Southampton where poverty, disease and crime were rife. A candle factory there boiled down animal carcasses to make tallow candles for the poor and the stench was overwhelming. The infant mortality rate in Southampton in the late 1800s was that 530 out of every 1,000 babies would not reach their fifth birthday. It was here that Ellen Wren lived, and her life was a sad story of violence, alcoholism, petty crime and prostitution. Her mother was a brothel keeper. Ellen Wren died of 'suffocation from excessive drinking' in a squalid attic room in Castle Court, Simnel Street, in 1894. She had choked on her own vomit after drinking 'mother's ruin' – gin. Nobody had

The Council House from *c.* 1902 above the medieval Undercroft and opposite the Titanic pub.

noticed the smell of a body decaying as the whole area had been described as unfit for human habitation. However, Ellen's difficult life did lead to some positive changes. The subsequent public outcry and a newspaper campaign prompted the clearing of the slums for new social housing. Some remaining examples, built around 1902, can be seen on the corner of Bugle Street above the medieval Undercroft and opposite the Titanic pub. There is a managed block of flats for young mothers in Westbrook Way, Swaythling, named after her, run by the Chapter One Christian housing charity.

Emily Davies (1830–1921)

Born in Carlton Crescent, Emily Davies was a campaigner for women's education and a suffragette. Emily was co-founder of Girton College, Cambridge, in 1869, which was the first women's college and the first female college to become coeducational in 1976. Her Welsh father, Revd John Davies, moved to Southampton in the 1820s to open a school. Emily moved to London after the death of her father in 1861. Emily Davies House, a Solent University 240-bed hall of residence, was named to commemorate her.

Lucia Foster Welch (1864–1940)

Lucia came to Southampton in 1903 and took a keen interest in local politics and social welfare issues. Elected a Conservative councillor in 1918, she chaired the Health Committee from 1924. Lucia was Southampton's first female councillor, alderman and mayor in 1927. Nationally, she was active in the suffragette movement, a member of both the Women's Social and Political Union and the National Union of Women's Suffrage

Born in Carlton Crescent, Emily Davies was a campaigner for women's education and a suffragist.

Societies. A Southampton Solent University hall of residence was named after her in 1995. Her house still stands in Oxford Street but does not have a blue plaque.

DID YOU KNOW?
Southampton was named 'Fittest City in the UK' by *Men's Fitness* magazine in 2006. The city's residents had a higher percentage of gym memberships, less heart disease and consumed less alcohol and junk food than any of its counterparts. Another report soon after, however, found it to be in the top three for 'fat cities'!

Elsie Sandell (1891–1974)

Elsie was one of Southampton's best-known local historians. She was a prolific writer, producing a number of books on the town's history, including *Southampton Cavalcade* and *Southampton Panorama*. In addition to her historical interests she was involved with a number of local organisations, including the YWCA and the Poor Ladies Fund charity. She sat on the Public Libraries and Museums Committee, and in 1953 she became the first person to receive the Southampton Publicity Club's award for 'Outstanding Service to the Town'. Elsie lived at Winn Road from 1923 to 1970, when she moved to a flat in Westwood Road. That year a block of flats in the Parkway, Bassett, was named Sandell Court in her honour. She has been criticised for being a storyteller not a serious historian. I received one of her books as a school prize as a nine year old and it helped develop my lifetime love of history, leading, indirectly, to me writing this book.

General Charles Gordon (1833–85)

Gordon was born in London but his father Lieutenant General Henry Gordon retired to Southampton in around 1857 and lived in Rockstone Place off the Avenue with his family. General Gordon, who never married, regarded the house as his home from that time until his death at Khartoum in 1885. There is also a Khartoum Road in Highfield and a Gordon

Avenue in Portswood. The simple monument to Gordon stands on a mound in the centre of Queen's Park. It is almost 20 feet high and consists of four columns of Aberdeen granite on a marble base. Gordon was a modest man and it is fitting there is no likeness of him. The park was extensively renovated in 2011.

Colonel Alexander Ross Clarke (1828–1914)

Alexander Clarke's house was in Carlton Crescent and he is primarily remembered for his Principal Triangulation of Britain. He also wrote an important book on geodesy (the mathematical study of the shape and area of the earth). Clarke, an officer of the Royal Engineers and employed by the Ordnance Survey (OS), was a great friend of General Gordon who lived near his home in Southampton. In 1841, OS had moved to an empty former barracks in London Road, Southampton, following a fire at its previous premises in the Tower of London. In 2000, OS appointed Vanessa Lawrence as its first female director general. She oversaw the move from its Maybush head offices to a new site at Adanac Park, just off the M271, before leaving in 2014.

Sir John Jellicoe (1859–1935)

Born in Southampton, Jellicoe lived at several addresses, including No. 1 Cranbury Terrace, and was educated at Banister Park School. Jellicoe controversially commanded the Grand Fleet at the Battle of Jutland in May 1916. The public wanted a major naval victory like Trafalgar; instead it was a stalemate clash of the dreadnoughts, and some thought him too cautious. However, the German High Seas Fleet retreated to port and never seriously engaged in battle again during the First World War. In November 1916 he was promoted to First Sea Lord, made a viscount in 1918 and Admiral of the Fleet in 1919. In 1929 Southampton awarded him the Freedom of the Borough.

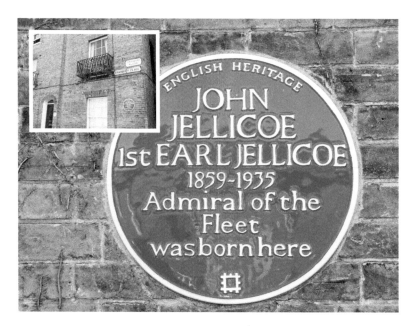

Southampton-born Jellicoe lived at several local addresses, including No. 1 Cranbury Terrace.

Bert Hinkler (1882–1933)

Hinkler was an Australian test pilot at Hamble and made many pioneering solo flights. In February 1928 he took sixteen days to complete the first solo flight from England to Darwin, Australia, in his Avro Avian. Bert lived at No. 39 Lydgate Road, Thornhill, at 'Mon Repos', which was named after a large turtle conservation park near his hometown of Bundaberg, Queensland, Australia. The nearby Hinkler pub on the Thornhill estate has some information on him. His house was completely dismantled in 1984 and transported to Bundaberg to be part of the Hinkler Hall of Aviation museum.

Isaac Watts (1674–1748)

Every four hours in daytime the Civic Centre bells play the tune 'St Anne' composed by organist William Croft. The words, based on Psalm 90, are by Watts – 'O God, Our Help in Ages Past' – and were originally published in 1719. Isaac was born in Southampton and his mother's nephew was Richard Taunton, the founder of the well-known Southampton school that is currently known as Richard Taunton Sixth Form College. The family lived at No. 41 French Street, where Isaac's father ran a boarding school. When Isaac was six years old he attended the 'Free School', later known as King Edward VI Grammar School. Watts House at the school is now named after him. Isaac then moved away to London to study at the Nonconformist Academy at Stoke Newington Green. Unhappy with the psalms and canticles that were sung, his father challenged him to do better. In 1707 he published *Hymns and Spiritual Songs*, which contains some of the most popular English hymns of all time. Isaac penned around 750 hymns, including 'There is a Land of Pure Delight' – it is said the words came to him while looking across the River Test towards the New Forest.

In 1707, Isaac Watts published *Hymns and Spiritual Songs*, which contains some of the most popular English hymns.

Quaker memorial stones are similar in size due to their belief that no one is more important than anyone else.

George Fox (1624–91)

In 1662, George Fox, founder of the Quakers, visited Southampton members of the Society of Friends of Truth. Some were in prison for holding illegal assemblies, refusing to doff their hats to the magistrates and refusing to attend their parish church services. Fox was the first to be called a Quaker after he had called on Justice Bennet to 'tremble at the name of the Lord'. Early meetings were held at the home of Captain George Embree who bought a £10 plot of pasture land by the Avenue on a thousand-year lease, which was given to the Quakers in 1709 for a peppercorn rent. Dissenters (as they were called), were not permitted to be buried in Anglican churchyards. Early Quaker graves were unmarked. Footstones (not headstones) were only allowed from the nineteenth century; the earliest surviving one is from 1817. All the later Quaker memorial stones are similar in size as they believe no one is more important than anyone else – in life or in death.

Walter Taylor III (1734–1803)

In October 1805, during the Napoleonic Wars, Admiral Nelson engaged thirty-eight Spanish and French ships off the coast of Spain near Cape Trafalgar. Having destroyed nineteen enemy ships, Nelson's victory ended Napoleon's plans to invade Britain and he became a national hero. It is little known, however, that his success at Trafalgar was in part due to the expertise of a Southampton father and son – both called Walter. At fourteen the young Walter was apprenticed to a ship's pulley block maker in Westgate Street, Southampton. At the time ship pulley blocks were not very reliable – as they were handmade individually there were variations in quality that could affect performance. Ships used the blocks to control the sails and to position cannons for firing. The Taylors bought a block-making business and developed machinery to mass produce their high-quality blocks, which proved to be so successful that the navy bought all the stock. Each British cannon could now fire as many as four volleys to the enemy's one in the same time. The father died in 1762 and young Walter continued mass-producing

Nelson's Trafalgar victory was aided by a Southampton father and son, both called Walter Taylor.

100,000 blocks a year for the Admiralty from 1759 until 1801. The business later moved to Mayfield Park in Southampton where a stream provided the power for the machinery. In 1781 the business moved to Woodmill where the water power was supplemented by steam engines. Taylor lived in Portswood Lodge on the site of the present library on Portswood Broadway. Southampton Art Gallery has a painting of a New Year's feast he provided for his employees. By 1801 the Admiralty were in discussion with Walter regarding new block-making machinery designed by Marc Brunel, father of Isambard Kingdom Brunel, which eventually meant manufacturing of the blocks was moved in-house to Portsmouth Dockyard in 1803. Walter is buried at South Stoneham Church.

Richard Andrews (1798–1859)

Richard Andrews, 'Southampton's Dick Whittington', was born near Alresford, around 20 miles north of Southampton. From eight to fourteen he was an under sawyer, walking the 10 miles to and from work. He became a coach maker's apprentice and at twenty-one

Richard Andrews was known as Southampton's Dick Whittington.

he walked to Southampton and found employment in a coach factory. Having saved £75 he set up business in October 1832, as a master coach maker with two workmen. By 1845 he earned more than £22,000, selling around 300 carriages and employing 200 men. He sold to the aristocracy and gentry, and he built three small carriages for Queen Victoria's use at Osborne House. A good employer, he was an active Liberal in local politics and was a five times Mayor of Southampton. When Richard Andrews died the pallbearers at his funeral were, at his request, twelve of his workmen who had been with him for twenty years. A statue of him, designed by fellow local Liberal Philip Brannon, was erected by public subscription in East Park. The foundation stone was laid on 1 October 1860 and 4,000 people assembled to see the ceremony.

King Canute/Cnut (995–1035)

Canute was king of Denmark, England and Norway. There is a 'Canute dispute' as several places, such as Bosham in West Sussex, claim to have been the location that he commanded the tide not to come in. Southampton, however, does in fact have a strong claim as he is said to have been crowned here. We even have a plaque on the Canute Hotel opposite the entrance to Ocean Village. It is generally agreed nowadays that, wherever he did it, the aim was to show that kings did not have the supernatural or divine power to control nature and were only human. His and Queen Emma's burial chest are in Winchester Cathedral.

William Cantelo (1830–*c*. 1885) and Hiram Maxim (1840–1916)

William Cantelo was an inventor said to be working on an early version of the machine gun. He left his Southampton home one day and never returned. Local residents had reported hearing the sound of rapid gunfire from a cellar beneath the former Bargate Street pub by Arundel Tower run by William Cantelo. Cantelo, an engineer and gunmaker, was experimenting with a machine gun. By the mid-1880s Cantelo went off with his invention, presumably to sell it. He frequently travelled far on sales trips as a successful builder of ships' capstans. In a strange coincidence, Cantelo was fond of quoting literary maxims and carried a book of them in his pocket. He was never seen again.

When the American inventor Sir Hiram Maxim died he was a rich man and a knight of the realm, having moved to England in 1900. Maxim had left America, where he had made enemies by arguing with Thomas Edison over who invented the light bulb. Maxim invented the mousetrap and also had invented his Maxim machine gun. But what happened to Southampton's William Cantelo? According to a 1930s 'Townsman' column in the local *Echo* newspaper, Cantelo's sons had seen a photo of Maxim that they thought was the image of their missing father. They tracked him down at Waterloo station, shouted 'Father!' and tried to approach him, but the train pulled away. Cantelo's family engaged a private detective to look for him, who traced him to America whereupon the trail went cold. In his autobiography Maxim complained of a 'double' who was going round the US

The 20-metre-high Arundel Tower was the north-west corner of the medieval town walls.

impersonating him. Was this Cantelo? Did Cantelo and Maxim ever meet? The daughter of another Southampton marine engineer wrote a letter telling how Maxim had come to Southampton to see a type of propeller her father had invented. He had told his staff not to show it to him because Maxim, she said, had a reputation of stealing ideas. So what did happen to William Cantelo? Did he realise he'd been pipped to the post by Maxim and come to a bad end trying to sell his own version of the gun? It is a real Victorian mystery.

The Slade Brothers

The Slade brothers missed the *Titanic* because, on the morning of 10 April 1910, they stayed too long at the Grapes pub, Oxford Street. The pub was not far from Dock Gate No. 4 and near to the White Star Dock (Berth 43/44), where she was due to set off on her maiden voyage at noon. On Friday 6 April 1912, the hiring of crew for *Titanic*'s voyage began. Alfred, Bertram and Thomas Slade were among them. They are recorded in *Titanic* crew records as all of them living at No. 21 Chantry Road, Southampton. Alfred (aged twenty-five), Bertram (aged twenty-six), and Thomas (aged twenty-seven) were all taken on as firemen. On sailing day the men reported at 8 a.m. for muster, after which they went ashore for a last drink – alcohol consumption on board was not allowed for crew. Two of these men were John Podesta and William Nutbeam. According to Podesta's account, they left to make their way back to the ship around 11.15 a.m. and stopped at the Grapes

The Slade brothers missed the *Titanic* as they stayed too long at the Grapes, Oxford Street.

for one more drink. They met up with the Slade brothers and other crew members. At around 11.50 a.m. Podesta, Nutbeam and the Slade brothers left the pub. As they were about to cross Canute Road a train was blocking their way. Podesta and Nutbeam quickly crossed, but by the time the rest of the group were able to cross the road it was 11.59 a.m. and *Titanic*'s gangway had been raised. Substitutes had been taken on who all perished when *Titanic* went down. Podesta and Nutbeam, however, survived. Those like the Slade brothers who had come aboard, stood muster, then left the ship but failed to return by sailing time were regarded by the White Star Line as 'deserted'.

Mary Anne Rogers (1857–99)

Mary was chief stewardess on the London & South Western Railway Company (LSWR, 1838–1922) cross-Channel mail and passenger boat, the *Stella* – the '*Titanic* of the Channel Islands'. When the boat sank, her last words were said to be, 'Goodbye, Goodbye, Lord have me.' She had refused to save herself, fearing she would capsize the overloaded lifeboat and gave up her own lifebelt.

Somerset-born Mary Anne had moved to Clovelly Road, Southampton, upon her marriage. She was six months pregnant with their second child when her seaman husband drowned at sea. The small pension forced Mary – now the breadwinner – to take up employment. Despite her continuing battle against seasickness, Mary became chief stewardess.

On 30 March 1899, Maundy Thursday, the first daytime sailing of the season, the *Stella* departed late. The *London Times* reported that the fierce competition between rival companies London & South Western Railway (LSWR) and the Great Western Railway

Mary's last words were said to be, 'Goodbye, Goodbye, Lord have me.'

(GWR) to arrive first was 'reckless and disgraceful, causing the Stella to founder on the Casquets rocks off of Alderney'. Despite Mary's efforts, eighty-six died and her body was never found, though the wreck of the *Stella* was found in 1973. The Portland stone memorial opposite Mayflower Park is named after the ship rather than the heroine Rogers. In 1997, however, her sacrifice was recognised by a memorial plaque unveiled in St Peter Port, Guernsey.

General Sir George Hewett (1751–1840)
The Hewett family were the last owners of the Freemantle Park estate before it became housing. Sir George came to Freemantle in 1822 after retiring from a distinguished army career. He was buried in the crypt of St James's Church, Shirley, with a memorial placed in the old St Nicholas Church, Millbrook. His name still lives on locally in Sir George's Road and Hewitts Road (although misspelt!).

Lieutenant General Henry Shrapnel (1761–1842)
The inventor of the shrapnel shell lived at Peartree House, near Peartree Green, from around 1835 until his death. Peartree House was built in the late 1500s and is now a care home. In 1814, the British government recognised Shrapnel's contribution by awarding him £1,200 (approximately £74,000 today) a year for life. Until the end of the First World War the shells were still manufactured according to his original principles.

General Juan Manuel de Rosas (1793–1877)
General de Rosas lived at Rockstone House, Carlton Crescent, before purchasing the 400-acre Burgess Street (today Burgess Road) Farm at the top of Langhorn Road, Swaythling. It is believed that he chose Southampton to live as it was near to the residence of Lord Palmerston, the foreign secretary and prime minister, who lived at Broadlands, Romsey. Palmerston has his own statue in the Above Bar, Southampton Central Park, named after him. De Rosas was born into a wealthy cattle-owning family descended from Spanish settlers in what is now Argentina. He used his private army to overthrow the Governor of Buenos Aires Province in 1829. Rosas took control of all aspects of government, formed a secret police and his portrait had to be displayed in public places. In 1852 his army was defeated by a coalition of Brazilian, Uruguayan and Argentines, and he fled on a British warship. He was buried at Southampton Old Cemetery, but his remains were repatriated in 1989 and buried in Buenos Aires in the same cemetery as Eva Peron. The general's daughter, son-in-law, granddaughter and youngest grandson remain buried at the Old Cemetery.

Flight Lieutenant James Nicholson (1917–45)
During action to the east of Southampton on 16 August 1940, Nicholson of 249 Squadron was badly wounded when his Hawker Hurricane was attacked by a Messerschmitt Bf 109. Despite his cockpit being on fire, he attacked and shot down a Bf 110 German fighter, suffering serious burns. Bailing out and landing in Redbridge, he was then mistakenly fired on by members of the Home Guard. His Hurricane crashed into what are now the grounds of Rownhams Junior School. There is a Hurricane Drive and Nicholson Walk nearby today.

Nicholson recuperated in Garton Ward at the Royal South Hants Hospital. For his actions he became Fighter Command's only recipient of the Victoria Cross during the Second World War. In 2016 a plaque to commemorate him was unveiled in Sholing Junior School by Don Smith, an eyewitness to the 1940 encounter. The plaque has the words of Winston Churchill: 'Never was so much owed by so many to so few.' Nicholson became wing commander of 27 Squadron in 1944 and died when a passenger in a Liberator crashed in the Bay of Bengal in May 1945.

Jack Mantle (1917–40)

Mantle was educated at Taunton School and was the only Southampton-born Victoria Cross recipient of the Second World War. Jack died manning an anti-aircraft gun on HMS *Foylebank* when it was under attack by German bombers in Poole Harbour. The VC is the highest award for gallantry in the face of the enemy that can be awarded to British and Commonwealth troops. A play area at the sports centre is named 'Jack's Corner' after him.

Lord Louis Mountbatten (1900–79)

A statue of Lord Mountbatten is in Southampton's Grosvenor Square. He was murdered by the IRA in August 1979. He lived at Broadlands estate in Romsey and was the Supreme Allied Commander in south-east Asia during the Second World War. In 1947 he was the last Viceroy of India before its independence and is buried in Romsey Abbey.

A statue of Lord Mountbatten in Grosvenor Square, Southampton.

Edwin Rowland Moon (1886–1920)

Edwin Moon's grave marker in Southampton Old Cemetery is said to be from the propeller of the plane in which he died. The aviation pioneer was born in Southampton and grew up in Cranbury Avenue. He designed and flew a monoplane – *Moonbeam II* – in 1910. It was the first plane to take off from what is today Southampton International Airport. He worked out of the family boat-building business at the former Wool House – now the Dancing Man Brewery pub. Squadron Leader Major Edwin Rowland Moon was in 230 Squadron, who flew reconnaissance flying boats from Felixstowe. At that time the squadron was known as the Royal Flying Corps or Royal Naval Air Force, which was part of the army before the formation of the RAF in April 1918 – hence his double ranking as major and squadron leader. Having survived the First World War, Edwin died in a flying accident and was buried with full military honours.

R. J. Mitchell (1895–1937)

R. J. Mitchell designed the iconic Second World War Spitfire fighter plane and lived in Portswood in a house he designed. The aeronautical engineer worked at the Supermarine Aviation Works in Woolston, which was destroyed by a Luftwaffe raid on 26 September 1940. A statue of Mitchell was installed at London Science Museum in 2005, but there is not one in Southampton. In 2004 a sculpture of the Spitfire was unveiled outside Southampton Airport.

In 2004 a sculpture of the Spitfire was unveiled outside Southampton Airport.

John Arlott (1914–91)

Later a cricket commentating legend, Sergeant John Arlott left Southampton Police in July 1945, having joined in 1934. He was to join the BBC on the recommendation of friend and fellow poet and writer John Betjeman. Arlott had moved to Howard Road, Shirley, with his first wife after serving during the Second World War in Special Branch screening aliens entering Britain. He also lived at No. 114 Lodge Road from 1943. St Luke's Church in Bevois Valley, now a Sikh place of worship, was where he married his first wife. According to Arlott's autobiography, when he left his wife, the straight-laced vicar wrote to him to saying curtly, 'I thought better of you!' Arlott wrote an illustrated book of twelve sonnets about Roman Southampton, 'Clausentum', which had drawings of Bitterne Manor House. John Arlott greatly admired England batsman Charles Burgess (known as C. B.) Fry (1872–1956) and wrote that he was 'probably the most variously gifted Englishman of any age'. Fry played cricket for Hampshire in 1920–21 and also played twenty-five times for Southampton FC, including the 1902 FA Cup final. Arlott's eldest son Jim was killed in a car accident on New Year's Eve 1965 driving home late at night from Southampton to Alresford in a sports car that Arlott had helped him buy. The tragedy led to Arlott always wearing a black tie in remembrance of his son. The University of Southampton has a bar and courtyard named after Arlott.

DID YOU KNOW?
Southampton won the 1976 FA Cup after beating Manchester United 1-0. The cup was presented by the Queen – the last time she was to do so. Bobby Stokes (1951–95), who scored the winning goal, was born in Portsmouth.

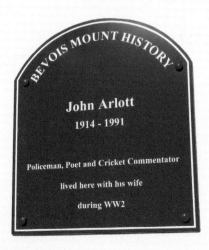

Arlott lived at No. 114 Lodge Road from 1943.

Heinz Burt (1942–2000)

Germany-born Heinz was a singer and bass player with a distinctive blonde hairstyle, He grew up in Eastleigh and died in Weston, Southampton. Heinz was a member of the Tornadoes who had a massive No. 1 hit in 1962 with the Joe Meek-produced instrumental 'Telstar'.

William Cobbett (1763–1835)

There is a plaque to William Cobbett in Botley, where he lived from 1805–35. Cobbett Road in Bitterne Park, Southampton, is named after the great radical agitator. The National Liberal Land Company, who developed the Bitterne Park estate, named many of its roads after nineteenth-century liberals and radicals. He visited Southampton on a number of occasions, some of which are described in *Rural Rides* (1816), a journal of his travels through the southern counties of England.

John le Fleming (1295–1336)

Fleming was a mayor and a parliamentary burgess for Southampton. The Fleming family can be traced back to 1217, when a Walter le Fleming was appointed Collector

Fleming was a medieval mayor and a parliamentary burgess for Southampton.

of the King's Prisage. This was the king's entitlement to claim for himself one in ten of the barrels of French wine imported into the town. The le Fleming family shield is among those awaiting restoration on the front of the Bargate. In 1620 the former Bull Hall, off Bugle Street, was let by the 3rd Earl of Southampton to a Sir Thomas Fleming, who married an aunt of Oliver Cromwell. His father, also Thomas, had been Lord Chief Justice of England and involved in the 1605 trial of Guy Fawkes and other Gunpowder Plot conspirators. Thomas Snr purchased the North Stoneham estate from the Earl of Southampton and died there in 1618. In 1825 a John Fleming bought Chilworth Manor, which was completely rebuilt by 1904 and is now a Best Western hotel. The Fleming estate once extended to around 15,000 acres of land in Hampshire and the Isle of Wight.

Charles Miller (1874–1953)

Charles William Miller was the man who introduced football to Brazil – the country has gone on to win the World Cup five times. He was born in São Paulo and his father was a Scottish railway engineer. In 1884 he was sent to Banister Court School in Southampton. Charles was a talented footballer, and in 1891, aged seventeen, he made his debut for Southampton St Mary's FC (later renamed Southampton FC) with his last appearance in the 1893/4 season. He returned to Brazil in 1894, reportedly carrying a Hampshire FA rulebook and two footballs, and set about introducing the game to the Brazilians.

This plaque to the public-spirited Edward is rather hidden in Palmerston Park.

Edward Chalk (1910–79)

There was a plan to take a sizeable area of the 365-acre common to create an extended car park for the Cowherds and to enable parking for supporters of the Southampton FC – they were newly promoted to the old Division 1 and in 1966 played home games at the nearby Dell ground. Edward Chalk opposed the plan and risked his home by using his house as security for legal costs. This plaque to the public spirited Edward is rather hidden in Palmerston Park.

Thomas 'Tommy' Lewis (1873–1962)

Tommy was a Southampton-born trade unionist, local councillor from 1901–61 and in 1929 the first Labour Member of Parliament for Southampton, along with Ralph Morley. Thomas Lewis Way and Thomas Lewis House in Empress Road are named after him. The Bevois Mount History group have put a plaque on the Alma Road house he lived in during his later years.

DID YOU KNOW?

'Dr Livingstone, I presume?' After the famous African explorer and missionary died, his body – minus his heart, which was left behind – arrived at the Royal Pier in Southampton in April 1874. It was taken in a procession through the town to the Terminus railway station to be taken to Westminster Abbey. A road in Portswood is named after him.

2. Secret Old Town Places

The Old Town was a network of courts, alleyways, overcrowded tenements and lodging houses, many of them with no windows or back door. There were open pits used as toilets, which were then covered with ash dust from your fire. At night a man that Victorians named as 'the Dustman' would come with his cart and remove the contents and dump it outside of the town. A drain at the bottom of Blue Anchor Lane was made by Harland and Wolff, who repaired ships in the docks between 1907 and 1973 and famously built the *Titanic* in Belfast. Drains and seats were made during quiet times. From the 1890s, the whole area was eventually cleared for new housing.

Royal Pier Pineapples
Why is a pineapple on top of our former Royal Pier entrance building? In 1493, Christopher Columbus had arrived on Guadalupe and his landing party came across a village. Outside the huts were fresh fruits, one of which was the *anana*, the Carib word for 'excellent fruit'. Columbus recorded it in his log as looking like a pine cone with the sweet flavour and firmness of an apple. By the 1660s, Charles II had posed for an official portrait of him receiving a pineapple. The trophy for the men's singles tennis at Wimbledon has a pineapple design that adorns the top of the lid. There was a tradition where captains in the British navy coming back from sea put a pineapple on the gateposts of their home to show that they 'at home' to visitors. Some older houses in Southampton still have stone pineapples on top of entrance gates. The pineapple has become a symbol of welcome, friendship, wealth and hospitality.

The Spire of St Michael's
The oldest Norman parts of the Grade I listed St Michael's Church date from 1070, making it the oldest building still in use in Southampton. The stained glass behind the altar dates from 1949 and shows the original five medieval parishes of Southampton, from left to right: St John the Baptist, St Laurence, St Michael, Holy Rood, and All Saints. In 1338 locals sheltered here during a raid by French and Genoese pirates. A slightly blackened wall to the right of the altar is said by some to be from a fire started by the pirates after they had slit the throats of those who came here for sanctuary, though this is probably a myth. The stained-glass window above the entrance was designed in 1951 by Southampton-born Noel Blay. It depicts St Michael fighting a dragon, who represents the Devil. St Michael, the patron saint of Normandy, is surrounded by shields, honouring local civilian groups involved on the home front during the Second World War. The church has a rare mid-fourteenth-century brass eagle lectern – probably the oldest brass one in England. It was rescued by the churchwarden from nearby

A pineapple on top of our former Royal Pier entrance building.

Holy Rood during a 1940 air raid. It was thought to be a wooden eagle until the brown paint was removed. The lectern may have been painted so Cromwell's men would leave it alone during the Civil War (1642–51).

There is an often-repeated local story that, during Second World War air raids, the Luftwaffe were told not to bomb St Michael's Church as its spire was a navigational aid. The spire of St Michael's Church was first added to the eleventh-century Norman church in the fifteenth century, and reconstructed in 1732. In 1887, to make it a better landmark for shipping, a further 9 feet was added to it on request from Trinity House. It is now 165 feet (50.29 metres) high. Steeplejacks traditionally leave information inside the body of the cockerel on top for future generations. This has been done in 1878, 1913, 1924 and 1968

The oldest building still in use in Southampton.

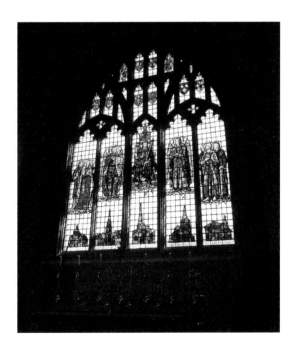

The stained-glass east window of St Michael's Church showing the five medieval parishes.

Built between 1491 and 1518, Tudor House became a museum in 1912.

when some pre-decimal coins were left inside. From September to December 1940 a series of raids by the German Air Force devastated Southampton. Many of the buildings in High Street and Above Bar Street were reduced to rubble. Many homes in Woolston, near the Supermarine Spitfire factory, were destroyed. There were 2,631 high-explosive and over 30,000 incendiary bombs dropped on the town, killing 631 people and injuring 19,000. Over 3,500 buildings were destroyed and 40,000 damaged. Today's planes can bomb very accurately, but Second World War air raids were less precise. Holyrood Church is very near St Michael's and also had a spire, but it was destroyed. It is almost certainly luck that St Michael's was not hit. A nearby bomb did blow out all of its windows, except the Lady Chapel ones. During a blackout the crew would not be easily able to see any spires, even if flares had been dropped. Nevertheless, the story persists and nearby Tudor House did survive wartime bombing when all other Southampton churches on medieval foundation did not.

DID YOU KNOW?
The first bomb fell on Southampton on 19 June 1940 and the last, a Doodlebug, on 15 July 1944. A total of 2,631 high-explosive bombs and 30, 652 incendiary bombs were recorded from around sixty raids, killing 631.

Back of the Walls

The eastern area of the Old Town, including the former fruit, vegetable and flower market, has recently been extensively redeveloped. It is known as the BOW development from Back of the Walls. Austen House has a series of granite slabs along the front entrance with engravings of medieval people and events. The BOW artwork is by Anna Vickers, who says:

> The artwork concept for the laser-engraved granite slabs is 'Meet the Locals', and depicts aspects of the lives of the working people, who would have made their homes around the area, and contributed to its prosperity. The wealthy merchants who traded in wine, the builders of the walls, the soldiers, sailors, craftspeople, and those involved in the production and trade of wool

The nearby Old Bond Store dates from the late 1700s. This was a bonded warehouse, a building where dutiable goods could be stored or undergo manufacturing operations without payment of duty. It is a lost building type for Southampton, where such stores were once commonplace.

The East Street car park, opposite the Bond Store, is on the site of the old All Saints' Church's nineteenth-century burial ground. In the early twentieth century the tombstones

The BOW development takes its name from the 'Back of the Walls'.

The nearby Old Bond Store dates from the late 1700s.

were removed and the land was a play area for children. All Saints' Church, destroyed during the Second World War, was at the High Street end of East Street. There is a Jane Austen plaque on the wall as she worshipped there when in Southampton.

The Chamberlayne Column

The once fashionable spa town of Southampton had streets lit up using coal gas from around 1820. William Chamberlayne MP donated the iron columns for the lights as long as the gas from his company was used. A surviving example can be seen inside Castle Vault on a guided tour with See Southampton. A column was erected in his honour in Above Bar Street in 1822, which was later moved to Town Quay and then to the roundabout by Debenhams. It is now in Houndwell Park, minus the original gold leaf that covered the dome at the top – it was removed some years ago after complaints from the people working in the former tax office in nearby Hanover Buildings, as the sun reflected off it through their windows. The flats in Britannia Road by St Mary's Football Stadium were built for the gas company workers in 1904.

The Bargate

The Bargate is the most recognisable symbol of Southampton, so not exactly a secret. Its oldest parts date from around 1180. Pevsner said that our Bargate is 'probably the finest and certainly the most complex town gateway in Britain'. Lots of notable events have

An 1822 column to William Chamberlayne was originally in Above Bar Street.

happened here. In the summer of 1415, Henry V was in Southampton preparing for a campaign in France when a plot against him, led by his cousin Richard, Earl of Cambridge, Lord Scrope of Masham and Sir Thomas Grey of Northumberland, was discovered. The conspirators were beheaded just north of the Bargate.

In 1592/3 Lord Strange's company of players performed here. One of their actors was William Shakespeare, but it is not known if he was actually in the group who visited Southampton on this occasion. It is possible, though, as the 3rd Earl of Southampton was a patron and Shakespeare dedicated several works to him. A 2016 play at the Nuffield Theatre was based on the premise that the two men had an intimate relationship.

Southampton has one of the few remaining court leet ceremonies left in England. It has its roots in Saxon law and is still held every October in the present council chamber. Anyone can make a 'presentment' on a local topic. If approved by court leet, the relevant council officer or department will send a written reply. The annual court leet was held in the Bargate's first floor – the Guildhall – until 1856. Until the Civic Centre law courts (now partly used by SeaCity Museum) were opened in 1933, the Guildhall was used as a courtroom with a police station next door – there are some visible carvings at the entrance to what was once the town jail.

On the south side of the Bargate is the statue of George III, dressed to impress as the Roman emperor Hadrian. It was presented to the town in 1809 by the Marquess of Lansdowne. It was made of artificial Coade stone (a mix of clay, terracotta, silicates and

The SeaCity Museum at the
Civic Centre.

glass) at the works in London run by Eleanor Coade, one of the few women to be a major influence on eighteenth-century architecture. It has lasted remarkably well for a statue well over 200 years old.

Once the only road route between Southampton High Street and Above Bar was through the arch in the centre of the Bargate. In 1923, a newly designed, enclosed, double-deck tram was introduced, which had a rounded top that would fit through the arch. Despite the clever design, the roadway through the arch in the Bargate still had to be lowered and some fine-tuning of the arch masonry was also required. A way was cleared for trams to pass around the east of the Bargate on 24 April 1932. The last tram to pass through the central archway did so on 4 June 1938, by which time some demolition work meant that the Bargate was now passable on both sides. This green stain is a reminder of the electricity cables that once powered the trams and touched against the stone.

The pavement plaques, from the Bargate down to the Town Quay, highlight some of the main events of the town in date order. At each stop, a plaque explains the event and there is another with an extract from writings of the period.

George III's head on the body
of the Emperor Hadrian.

Bargate south view. Its oldest
parts date from around 1180.

The green stain was caused by
electric tram cables.

Above left: Two lions guard the north entrance of the Bargate.

Above right: The first pavement plaque on the south side of the Bargate.

Old Town Walls and Vaults

The respected architectural historian Sir Nikolaus Pevsner (1902–83) is best known for his forty-six-volume series of county-by-county guides, *The Buildings of England*. Pevsner said of Southampton's walls: 'In all Britain there are few, if any, examples of medieval urban defences as impressive as those in Southampton.' The walls were completed around 1400. They extended over a distance of a mile and a quarter and originally contained seven principal gateways and twenty-nine towers. They are built mainly of Isle of Wight limestone, and some a better quality French stone from Caen. They are around 2 metres thick and their height varies from approximately 4 metres up to 9 metres in places.

Around half of the walls remain today, mainly on the western side, which was once the shoreline of the former Western Bay. Following the attack by French and Genoese raiders in 1338, walls were constructed along the West Quay where the traders had homes and warehouses – some windows and doors are still visible in the stretch known as the Arcades. The west gate was the last to be built at the end of the fourteenth century, and it was designed have cannon.

Estimates vary from forty-eight to eighty plus as to how many vaults Southampton had. Today a limited number are safe to enter on a guided tour. They were mainly built to store wine from Gascony during the Plantagenet era and stay at a constant temperature all year of around 11 °C or 52 °F.

In 1386, Richard II (1367–99) appointed the cleric Thomas Tredington to conduct religious services in Southampton Castle. Thomas's role was important as he was also keeper of the castle, and of the king's weapons and artillery inside. This arrangement was continued by Henry IV in 1399. The footsteps near Catchcold Tower are a reminder of his daily journey from the castle to the Catchcold Tower – one of the last additions to the western walls and housed a defensive cannon.

The Polymond drum tower was partly ruined in 1828/29 when the upper part was removed. John Polymond was an MP and several times Mayor of Southampton during the late 1300s.

Tredington's walk to Catchcold Tower from the castle.

The building known as King John's Palace can be seen from the garden of Tudor House. This building is believed to be the oldest Norman building in the country. The medieval chimney was moved there following Second World War bomb damage to its original site nearby.

The Red Lion in the High Street contains a Norman cellar, a Norman chimney breast and claims numerous ghosts. The courtroom is often said to be the scene of the trial of the conspirators against Henry V in 1415. However there is no existing documentary evidence I am aware of to support this belief. The trial would almost certainly have taken place in the former Southampton Castle.

Holy Rood

Hold Rood was built on its present site in 1320. Prince Philip of Spain heard Mass here upon his arrival in Southampton in 1554, before riding to Winchester to marry Henry VIII's daughter Mary (1516–58), who became queen in 1553. The site fell victim to bombing in 1940 and since 1957 it has been a memorial to the merchant navy, as shown by the 'MN' above the entrance.

The storm petrels on the gate in front of the altar were known as the sailor's friend. As bad weather approached they gave warning by circling a ship and then heading to shore. Outside on the pavement are some gannet seabirds. Superstitious sailors felt they represented the souls of sailors lost at sea. The *Titanic* memorial inside was moved here in 1971 from its original site on the common. It is rather poignant as it was built from subscription by the poor families of the town who had lost men who worked as crew, often below deck.

Quarterjacks strike the quarters of each hour.

Above left: The 'MN' above the entrance gate of the 'Sailor's Church'.

Above right: The storm petrels on the gate in front of the altar were known as the sailor's friend.

The wooden quarter jacks in the tower were mentioned in 1760 and strike every fifteen minutes.

Holy Rood was once regarded as the town church and the mayor would worship here. There was a canopy front facing the High Street that was used for public notices that was called Proclamation House. The area outside was known into the twentieth century as 'the Asphalt' and locals would congregate here to see in the New Year.

A Church, Bank and Pub

The Standing Order pub is on the site of the former St Laurence's Church (interchangeably spelt Lawrence), which was demolished in 1925. The current building was occupied by Barclays Bank, hence the name, before becoming a Wetherspoons public house. It was one of Southampton's original five medieval parish churches and existed in the early years of the reign of Henry II, who was crowned in 1154. The medieval St Laurence's Church was pulled down in 1839 and rebuilt in 1842.

Agincourt Archer

The Agincourt Archer is by Challis Court on the Holyrood estate. Henry V's archers left through Southampton's west gate to fight in the Battle of Agincourt in 1415. Legend has it that this led to the rude two-finger 'V' sign. It is said that the French would cut off

Above: Remaining church wall on the side of the Standing Order pub.

Left: Archers were crucial to the English victory at the Battle of Agincourt in 1415.

two fingers from a captured archer so they could not shoot arrows again. In victory, the English archers made the very visible gesture of raising their fingers at the French. While this is an oft-repeated tale, it is most likely a twentieth-century myth.

High Street Coaching Inns

The Star Hotel is a good example of a Georgian coaching inn and still has the archway through which coaches passed in and out. An old notice reads: 'Coach to London, Sundays excepted, Alresford, Alton. Performs 10 hours.'

Princess Victoria (1819–1901) once stayed at the Star as a fourteen-year-old with her mother before she became queen in 1837.

The Dolphin dates from at least 1454. During Southampton's spa town period (1750–1820) the Dolphin became a social centre for the people who came to bathe on the Western Shore and drink the waters from the chalybeate spring. Its Georgian bow windows are believed to be the largest in England. Novelist Jane Austen (1775–1817) lived nearby in Castle Square from 1806–09. Jane attended winter balls held in the first-floor rooms – now named after her. The author of *Vanity Fair*, William Makepeace Thackeray (1811–63), stayed at the Dolphin too.

Castle Square

Jane Austen lived at a previous building on the Juniper Berry pub site in Castle Square with her brother, sister and mother from 1807–09. The house was rented from the Marquess of Lansdowne, who lived opposite in his mock-Gothic castle, which only lasted from 1805–15 and was built on the site of a previous Norman castle. The Juniper Berry was once a favourite of merchant seamen. Live entertainment in the 1970s included acts such as Dockland Doris. It was known as the Castle Tavern from 1986 to 1993, then as The Bosun's Locker until 2011 when it reverted to its original name. The nearby Old Court

Above: An old notice reads: 'Coach to London, Sundays excepted, Alresford, Alton. Performs 10 hours.'

Right: The Georgian bow windows at the Dolphin are believed to be the largest in England.

The mythical unicorn has been a Scottish symbol of purity and power since the 1300s.

House was built in 1852 in Castle Lane. The national animal of Scotland, the Unicorn, was considered dangerous by the English and can be seen chained with English lion wearing a crown on the left. Since the reign of Robert III of Scotland in the 1300s, the mythical unicorn has been used as a Scottish symbol of purity and power and was said to be the first animal to leave the Garden of Eden with Adam and Eve.

Queen's Park

Queen's Park is located opposite Dock Gate 4. The 5 acres of land was a gift to Queen Philippa from her husband Edward III (1312–77) following a major French raid on Southampton in October 1338. Philippa's chaplain, Robert de Eglesfield, founded Queen's College, Oxford, in her name in 1341 and God's House and its lands were transferred to the College. In 1504 it was assigned as Lammas land, which meant that from 6 April (the Purification) until 12 August (Lammas Day) the owners could plant and harvest crops. After Lammas Day the land became common grazing land. One prominent group who grazed their horses there were the select group of seven porters who loaded and offloaded wine from the merchants' ships. The meadow became popularly known as Porter's Mead as they kept their horses there.

Following the arrival of the railway from London and the growth of the docks, the 1844 Marsh Act was passed, which enabled the Corporation to sell or lease the marsh common land for building and to use the revenue to lay out the central parks. A further

The raised platforms are to give a view of where the *Titanic* sailed from in 1912.

The baths were an unsuccessful venture late in the spa town period.

The green was established for the use of the Warden of God's House Hospital.

Act of Parliament in 1884 enabled the conveyance of Porter's Meadow by lease to the Corporation from Queen's College for a perpetual yearly rent of £12, and in 1885 Queen's Park was created.

The raised areas opposite Queen's Park on Canute Road are viewing platforms to enable a view of the berth where the *Titanic* sailed from on 10 April 1912. The original garden was in remembrance of Alderman Vokes, the town's sheriff in 1926.

The front face of the Gloucester Baths also survives today as the façade of the former Union Castle House. These baths were an unsuccessful venture late in the spa town period, only lasting for twelve years from 1826.

The people of Southampton once joked that they could set their watches by the Union Castle Line, whose ships departed for South Africa on a Thursday at four o'clock precisely. Containerisation and the growth of air travel was to eventually catch up with the company. On 2 September 1977, after 110 years, the *SA Vaal* was the last Union Castle ship to leave Southampton.

MV *Calshot* and Calshot Spit Lighthouse

The *MV Calshot* tug tender was built in 1929 by J. L. Thornycroft at Woolston, as was the lighthouse ship on the right in 1914. It was designed for service at Calshot Spit at the entrance to Southampton Water to act as a guiding light to the ships and flying boats and to warn of sandbanks. Both are now moored alongside Ocean Terminal.

The MV *Calshot* tug tender and *Calshot Spit* by Ocean Terminal.

A possible cannon that may have been shot in the wall by Cuckoo Lane near the *Mayflower* monument.

Cuckoo Lane Cannon Shot

A cannon was possibly shot in the wall by Cuckoo Lane, just west of the bottom of Bugle Street and near the *Mayflower* monument. When Henry V lay siege to Harfleur during the 1415 Agincourt campaign he had cannon that would fire 12-inch-diameter stone cannonballs carved on the Isle of Wight. There are several theories as to their origin. In the late fourteenth century, when the town defences were being strengthened, were some spare cannonballs used to help complete the wall? Could they be trebuchet missiles dredged out of Town Quay? Or are they just naturally occurring rocks dredged from Southampton Water and put there more recently?

Garderobe

The Garderobe was a toilet for the medieval Southampton Castle, which was in use until the early 1600s. The double tide that came up to the western walls helped flush waste out to sea. People – old, young, male and female – would sit openly together and not in cubicles. They would discuss matters of interest and some say this is where the phrase 'doing your business' originates.

The water once came up to the western walls.

The Masonic Hall at Forty Steps

The Masonic Hall in Albion Place overlooks the new part of the Westquay development and has been hosting meetings since 1879. A founder was James Lemon, who was the borough engineer, twice mayor and has a road in Shirley named after him. Many nineteenth-century Southampton mayors were masons, as was the architect Josiah George Poole. In December 1879 it was opened with a masonic ceremony, followed by a banquet at the Royal Victoria Rooms, which were situated on Portland Terrace. Opposite the Masonic Hall are the Forty Steps, which were built in the early 1850s to enable access to the then waterfront, which came up to the western walls. The area is very different now after around 400 acres were reclaimed from the sea from 1927–34 to build the Western Docks.

DID YOU KNOW?
The Admiral Sir Lucius Curtis pub is by the entrance to Ocean Village. In 1838 he laid the foundation stone for the building of the new Eastern Docks.

3. More Secret Places

The Mayflower Theatre

This theatre was originally built in 1928 by the Moss Group as the Empire and had a roof terrace garden. It was then the Gaumont from 1950 to 1987, when it became the Mayflower. It reopened in September 2018 after a major refurbishment. Julie Andrews made her stage debut there as a ten-year-old in 1945. Ted and Barbara Andrews introduced their ten-year-old daughter who stood on a box to join her father at the microphone and sing. Laurel and Hardy and the Beatles performed there, and in October 1952 world-famous ballerina Dame Margot Fonteyn (1919–91) was due to dance. The Sadlers Wells Ballet prima ballerina complained of a sore throat while performing and went to the Southampton Chest Hospital in Millbrook to be treated for diphtheria. She spent two weeks in a glass isolation cubicle. The show was cancelled and the theatre had to be fumigated when the infection was discovered. Hollywood actress Bette Davis (1908–89)

The 1928-built Mayflower Theatre had a roof terrace garden.

was on a talk tour in the 1970s. She described Southampton in unequivocal tones from the stage, saying 'what a dump' – she had a point. The post-war rebuilding was functional. Today much of that has come to the end of its life and the city is being regenerated with numerous redevelopment projects.

Empire Gents Barber

Greek Cypriot George ran the popular Empire Gents Hairdressing for many years, until his passing in 2014. A well-known local character, he had two premises in Commercial Road. The original Empire barbershop (currently called Yuri) was opposite the Mayflower Theatre (originally the Empire) on the corner of Water Lane. He then moved further down toward the Central railway station opposite Wyndham Court and Nelson Gate. He was an engaging barber who let you make your own tea or coffee in the shop. George enjoyed telling interesting stories of famous people, such as Tony Curtis, he gave a haircut to while working on the liners. He would often open early – around 6.30 a.m. – to enable people catching an early train to get a haircut. The barber shop still keeps the Empire name.

Emperia Ruins

In 2018 Southampton City Council redeveloped the area of Blechynden Park, near Southampton Central railway station. A wall within the park remains from the site of the Emperia factory, which was built in 1905. This housed the Idris Mineral Water company, then British American Tobacco. It was bombed during a German raid in the Southampton

In 2018, Southampton Council redeveloped the area of Blechynden Park.

Blitz of 1940. There are very few explicit reminders in the city that link back to the Blitz and this park was deliberately kept as an undeveloped bomb site as a reminder to future generations. The new 4.9-metre corten steel arch represents the city's enduring strength and resilience in the face of fifty-seven Second World War air attacks that left nearly 45,000 buildings damaged or destroyed.

Manchester Street

Inside the Marlands shopping centre is a replica of Manchester Street. In 1982, the Environment Secretary, Michael Heseltine, turned down a council bid for a compulsory purchase to demolish this street. Despite this, in 1988 developers bulldozed the street because it was deemed 'structurally unsound'. The replica in Marlands is a reminder of the thriving nineteenth-century terrace that was once there.

The Cowherds

If you lived in the medieval town and owned a cow you could pay the cowherd to take her to the common to graze. He would collect the animals from outside the Bargate and herd them up to the land that was owned by Lord Shirley. The town burgesses found against him in a land dispute in the 1200s and it was given to the people to graze their livestock and to collect firewood, berries and peat. It is known as the common and it is managed

Inside the Marlands is a replica of Manchester Street.

by the council on behalf of all local people. It is still forbidden to build on it. In 1767 the building we know today as the popular Cowherds pub was built.

OSH 1T

A yellow Mini with an interesting number plate – OSH 1T – has been on display on the wall at Jarvis's garage in Bevois Valley since the early 1980s.

Lumpy Lane

At the rear of Northam Social Club, this Billy Mather mural is on what may be Southampton's shortest road. It once was 'unmade', so perhaps that explains the name.

An interesting number plate.

On the rear wall of Northam Social Club.

Antelopes and an Alien

William Dibben & Sons Ltd were a once well-known local builders' merchants. They had premises at Antelope Buildings by the former Antelope Sports Ground, north of Charlotte Place in St Mary's Road, near where the Jury's Inn is today. The ground was opposite the Antelope Inn, later Antelope Hotel, at No. 66 St Mary's Road, near the Brinton's Terrace entrance to the Royal South Hants Hospital. Until 1884 this ground was the home of Hampshire Cricket Club, and Southampton St Mary's played some of their early football games there until 1897. Today there is an adult mental health unit called Antelope House on part of the site. Dibben later moved to new premises on Bursledon Road, Thornhill. This is now called Antelope Park. There is a green alien 'We come in peace' statue there designed in 2009 by Dorset artist David Worthington.

DID YOU KNOW?
The Old Bowling Green in Lower Canal Walk claims to date from 1299, making it the oldest in England.

Sign on the former Antelope Building in St Mary's Road.

The 'We Come in Peace' green alien.

St Denys

St Denys Priory was built in 1124 during the reign of Henry I and closed by Henry VIII in 1536. An archway from the priory can be seen today in the garden of Tudor House in Bugle Street. A remnant of the priory's wall can be seen in the back garden of a house in Priory Road – it is covered in ivy, which cannot be removed as it may damage it. It is said that this stretch of fourteenth-century wall was saved as a consequence of the unexplained deaths of farm animals at the time; however, the priory's destruction was blamed as the cause of the deaths.

The growth of St Denys as a Victorian model suburb reflects the population growth of Southampton from around 10,000 in 1801 to 45,000 in 1851. There was a need to address overcrowding and public health problems in the town slums. The docks had opened and the railway had reached Southampton by 1840. Between 1840 and 1870 ten new churches were built in Southampton, including the St Denys Church (1868), named after the saint of the nearby priory. The Grade II listed church was designed in the French Gothic style by the renowned architect Sir George Gilbert Scott (1811–78), who also designed St Pancras railway station, the Albert Memorial and Westminster Abbey. Today the church is home to a restored seventeenth-century church organ, which may have been played by Handel. The many stained-glass windows include one detailing the First World War exploits of Daniel Beak VC, who lived with his family in Kent Road. The Board School opposite was opened in 1881.

A railway station was constructed in 1858 where St Denys Road crosses the railway today. It was officially opened in 1861 and named Portswood. The same year an Act was passed for the construction of a railway from Southampton Docks to the new Royal Victoria Military Hospital at Netley. Portswood station was closed and moved to the present site at the junction of the new line and renamed St Denys. The Netley branch line opened in 1866 and is said to contain one of the tightest bends on the railways. The original railway bridge over the River Itchen remains to this day.

Franciscan Friary

The Franciscan Friary was founded *c.* 1233 adjacent to God's House Tower. The friars laid a system of water pipes from a spring off Hill Lane, Shirley, to the friary, which was also used by Southampton residents. The Conduit House, almost opposite the Mayflower Theatre, was part of the water system.

DID YOU KNOW?
God's House Tower, on the corner of Town Quay, Lower Canal Walk and Platform Road, was built around 1417. It is the first dedicated artillery fortification built in England.

The Polygon

The original Polygon development was begun in 1768, designed to be a 'leisure complex' of hotels, properties to rent, restaurants and a dance hall. Only three buildings were ever completed. It was too far from the town centre for the wealthy to risk the dangerous journey, and was later the site of the Polygon Hotel. The current buildings have some original plaques on a front wall. The designers of the present flats in the site have made a nod to the original name in the multi-sided design of part of the top storey.

Golden Tooth

The Golden Tooth is outside No. 56 Bedford Place. Dentist Clive Marks has a practice at the north end of Bedford Place in a bow-fronted building dating from 1826. It has the country's only 'Golden Tooth' hanging on its façade, which had restoration work carried out on it in 2018.

The Fairy Village

These models were made in the 1940s by Mr Butler in his garden shed in Honeysuckle Road, Bassett Green. He moved to Burgess Road, Swaythling, in the 1950s and placed the models in his front garden, where they have been enjoyed by generations of children on their way to and from school. Wooden moulds had cement poured into them to form the walls of each building. Mirrors were placed inside so that the windows appear to light up.

Left: The Golden Tooth had restoration work carried out on it in 2018.

Below: The Fairy Village has been enjoyed by generations of children on their way to and from school.

Broadway Cinema

Situated on the Broadway, Portswood Road, the 1,500-seat Broadway Cinema opened in June 1930. It had King Arthur and Camelot decor with paintings of medieval knights and castles. The cinema survived the war undamaged, but was converted to a bingo club in the 1960s. Still visible on the side is some graffiti from when it was a cinema – some people would carve their names while queuing to get in. Today it is the Victory Centre Baptist Church.

DID YOU KNOW?
The *Two Figures* sculpture by Barbara Hepworth can be found at the Highfield Campus of the University of Southampton. The campus was designed by Sir Basil Spence in 1956.

Valley Gardens

The pleasant University of Southampton Highfield Campus is complete with streams and wildlife. Tucked away behind the sports hall is a delightful botanical garden on the site of a former brickworks. Students are often surprised to discover its existence, despite walking near it every day. Once inside the tranquil secret garden, which dates back to the 1940s, the bustle of modern life seems worlds away.

This peaceful garden dates from the 1940s.

International Towers

The 1960s-built International Towers in Weston are a familiar landmark to those who travel Southampton Water or look over from Hythe, but many may not realise they have names. They are, from left to right: Hampton, Havre, Oslo, Copenhagen, Rotterdam and Canberra.

DID YOU KNOW?
The tallest habitable building in Southampton is the Moresby Tower in Ocean Village at 262ft/80m.

There are also International Towers in California, Abu Dhabi and Sydney.

The twenty-four-storey, 70-metre-tall Canberra Towers dates from 1967.

The Moresby Tower is 80 metres (262 feet) tall, currently the highest residential building.

4. Secret Stories

No Grave but the Sea

It would be impossible in a book about Southampton not to mention the *Titanic*, which departed from the city's docks on 10 April 1912. The local impact was considerable as of the 724 local crew members the ship was carrying, 549 died in the disaster. Many of them came from the poorer areas of Chapel, Northam, St Mary's, Freemantle, Old Town and Oxford Street and had nobody to pay to bring their bodies home. This is powerfully illustrated by a large map within the floor of a large room at SeaCity Museum that has a red dot for each address affected by a loss. The rescue ships arrived with wooden coffins for first-class passengers, sacks for second-class, and for the crew a sack and a steel rod to weigh them down. The cable layer Mackay Bennett collected the bodies of *Titanic* crew members and there were 166 sea burials. None of the local crew that died in the disaster are buried in Southampton; however, the old cemetery on the common does have over sixty plots marked with a blue stick of people with a connection to the ship who died later. Recently, some plaques have been put on the homes of local crew who perished.

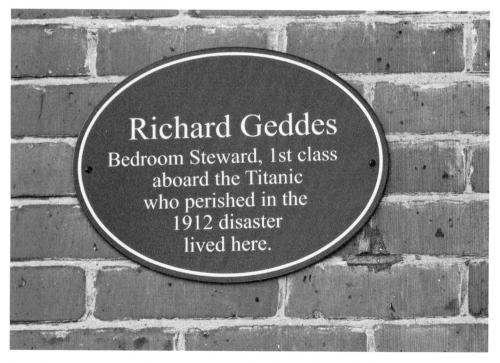

Recently some plaques have been put on homes of local crew who perished.

Titanic stevedore on the Holy Rood estate.

The goddess Nike at the memorial for the *Titanic* engineers.

The Titanic pub, with Castle Way flats behind.

Albert Road Chapel has been split in two since the construction of the Itchen Bridge in 1976. In 1912 this road connected the chapel area with the docks. The Atlantic Hotel on Albert Road South has now been converted into flats and apartments. Located a short walk up Canute Road and far removed from the opulence of the South Western Hotel where the rich and famous stayed, this building was where many of the *Titanic*'s third-class passengers stayed, as it provided cheap accommodation. Others stayed at the Alliance Hotel in Oxford Street, now called the White Star Tavern after the shipping line. Named the Titanic since the centenary in 2012, this Simnel Street pub has had a number of prior names – the Endeavour, Atlantic Queen, Queen of Clubs, and originally the Queen (this one can still be seen in some of the windows).

The Oakley & Watling Co. supplied fruit and veg supplies to ships, including the *Titanic*. Fruits can be seen on its façade. It closed in 1975.

Oakley & Watling supplied fruit and veg to the *Titanic* and other ships.

A ceremony at Southampton's mother church – St Mary's – to dedicate the Titanic Memorial Window was held in May 2018. Designed by Louise Hemmings, it features an angel holding a scroll remembering the crew and the quotation, 'Many waters cannot quench love'. There is one bubble for every member of the ship who died. The docks were very quiet in 1911/12 due to a coal strike depriving ships of their power source. Local historian Genevieve Bailey recounted how before the *Titanic* sailed many hungry men, who had been seeking aid, came to the church and said, 'We'll trouble you no more. Tomorrow we're off on the big one.' The British Titanic Society raised £20,000 towards the cost of the window.

The *Titanic*'s lookout at the time of the collision with the iceberg was Fred Fleet (1887–1965). He was one of the crew who survived and later lived in Freemantle. His former house is called the Lookout. Fleet told the *Titanic* inquiry that he and his lookout mates were disappointed not to receive any binoculars for the journey. In later years he sold the local *Echo* newspaper in Southampton. He is thought to have felt responsible for the sinking and loss of life that followed. The death of his wife greatly affected Fred, and he took his life by hanging soon afterwards. Frederick Fleet was buried without a headstone in Hollybrook Cemetery in Southampton in 1965. It remained unmarked until 1993, when the United States-based Titanic Historical Society funded a headstone. Some felt this was not appropriate, however, as it put Fred on the *Titanic* tourist trail.

Lookout sign on Fred Fleet's former house in Freemantle.

Is it SS or RMS *Titanic*? Some say that the *Titanic* was not fully a royal mail ship, as intended, but remained only a steamship. It left Southampton on 19 April 1912, but sank on the night of the 14/15 April before delivering its post, so some say it remains just the SS *Titanic*.

Millvina Dean was the youngest passenger on board at just two months old. She was also the last remaining survivor. She died in 2009 at the age of ninety-seven at a care home in Ashurst, near Southampton. Her ashes were scattered from a launch in the docks where the *Titanic* set sail. There is a small memorial garden named after her located to the side of the SeaCity Museum.

DID YOU KNOW?
The *Mayflower*, which brought the Pilgrim Fathers to America, set sail from Southampton. There were, in fact, two ships, the *Mayflower* and the *Speedwell*, which left Southampton together in August 1620. The *Speedwell* was left behind in Plymouth, however, as it was leaking.

The original memorial to the *Titanic* musicians was destroyed by bombing.

REPLICA OF THE MEMORIAL TO THE MUSICIANS OF THE S.S. TITANIC ORIGINALLY SITUATED IN THE VESTIBULE OF THE CENTRAL FREE LIBRARY WHICH OCCUPIED THIS SITE 1893-1940

The band are said to have played as the ship went down.

Edgar Allan Poe, Richard Parker, Cannibalism and the *Life of Pi*

In 1838, American author Edgar Allan Poe published *The Narrative of Arthur Gordon Pym of Nantucket*. Pym is one of four men stranded in a lifeboat and starving. Sixteen days in, one of the men proposes that one of them must die to preserve the others. Lots are made, and it is agreed that the man who draws the short straw will die. Ironically, it is the very man who argued first for cannibalism who draws the short straw and becomes the victim; his name was Richard Parker, who Pym thinks resembles a tiger.

The yacht *Mignonette* was built in 1867 and she was later purchased by John Henry Want, a wealthy Australian, who then needed crew to sail it to Australia. Before embarking on the voyage, she was to be made ready in Southampton for her long journey. One of her crew was seventeen-year-old Richard Parker from Itchen Ferry village. The long voyage began in May 1884. On 5 July the yacht foundered in a storm off Tristan da

Sacred to the memory
Richard Parker
Who died at sea July 25 ...
nineteen days dreadful suffering in an
open boat in the Tropics, having been
wrecked in the yacht Mignonette

———

Though he slay me, yet will I trust in Him
Job 13 v 15

Lord, lay not this sin to their charge
Acts 7 v 60

———

and of Sarah Parker
Died 6th January 1898 Aged 68

Richard Parker memorial stone at Pear Tree Church.

Cunha and the four crew members escaped in a lifeboat with two tins of turnips and no water. After twenty days they were drinking their own urine. Cabin boy Richard Parker, the seventeen-year-old from Itchen Ferry village, had lapsed into a coma – probably from drinking sea water. Skipper Tom Dudley decided that Parker should be killed and eaten to keep the others alive. Their reasoning was that they were family men and Parker was an orphan. Dudley cut the boy's throat with a penknife and he and Stephens, plus fourth crew member, Edmund Brooks, ate the boy's flesh. The surviving crew members lived off Parker's body and blood for the next four days before being rescued by the German ship *Moctezuma*. They were described in the press as 'living skeletons' and were landed at Falmouth. Dudley and Stephens were truthful on their return about killing Parker to stay alive, saying it was a 'custom of the seas', but they were charged with murder. Tom Dudley and Edwin Stephens were convicted of murder and sentenced to hang. The judge ruled that 'necessity was no defence for murder' and the 'custom of the seas' was abolished. The two men faced the death penalty, but there was much sympathy for them. The sentence was commuted to six months in prison by Queen Victoria. A memorial stone to Richard Parker was placed in Peartree Churchyard and can still be seen in the church's entrance. Another memorial is in the grounds.

More recently, Yann Martel released the book *Life of Pi* in 2001, which was made into a film in 2012. Pi's companion throughout his ordeal at sea is Richard Parker, a 450-pound royal Bengal tiger. Alone on the lifeboat, Pi has many issues to face, including lack of food and water, predatory marine life, treacherous seas and exposure to the elements. Pi must perform many actions to stay alive that he would have found unimaginable in his normal life. An avowed vegetarian, he must kill fish and eat their flesh. Having killed his mother's murderer, Richard Parker is the version of himself that Pi has invented to make his story more palatable to himself and to his audience. I have read that Yann Martel was aware of the Edgar Allen Poe story, but have not found out if he knew the sad story of Southampton's young Richard Parker.

DID YOU KNOW?
Red Funnel Ferries, who connect Southampton to the Isle of Wight, have possibly the longest company name in the UK: The Southampton, Isle Of Wight and South of England Royal Mail Steam Packet Public Ltd Co.

The Boat that Does not Float
This self-built boat is in a garden in Avon Road, Midanbury. It was started there in the 1960s and is a well-known local landmark. The owner is elderly now and it is doubtful if his dream boat will ever be realised.

The boat that does not float.

The Rabbit Woman

There is a print in the Giddy Bridge pub in London Road that depicts a Swiss royal physician named Nathaniel St André (1680–1776) who retired to nearby Bellevue House in 1750. He was a lifelong friend of poet Alexander Pope (1688–1744), who often stayed at nearby Bevois Mount House. He was appointed surgeon to the court of George I in 1723, and in 1726 examined a woman from Godalming named Mary Toft who claimed she had given birth to fourteen rabbits. St André was convinced the woman was telling the truth and he took her on a promotional tour and published a book on the story. When the con was exposed after Toft's confession, the doctor was disgraced and ruined.

Warrior – Southampton's Warhorse

On 22 August 1935 a much-loved Southampton Police Force horse died. Warrior was a warhorse who served on the Western Front in the First World War and was wounded at Mons in 1914. Warrior eventually returned to Britain in February 1919 and was sent to the Veterinary Field Hospital at Swaythling. Warrior is buried at the municipal golf course. Miss Hilda Moore purchased the grey gelding in 1919, named him Warrior and presented him to the Southampton Police Force. Her only condition was that once a year in May, Warrior be returned to her so that she could throw a party in his honour and give him sugar. Wearing his silver Mons Star, Warrior was ridden by Mayor Sidney Kimber during the peace celebrations of 1919.

Southampton's warhorse, Warrior, is buried at the municipal golf course.

Long Live Dubcek

This 'Long Live Dubcek' graffiti is still just visible after fifty years. Alexander Dubček (1921–92) was a Slovak politician who served as the leader of the former Czechoslovakia from January 1968. He attempted to reform the communist government during the Prague spring, but was forced to resign following the Russian Warsaw Pact invasion in August 1968.

In that Number

The history of Southampton FC is well documented elsewhere. It was a club built on faith from the start, as it began in 1885 as a team based on St Mary's Church – hence their nickname of 'the Saints'. The present St Mary's Stadium is very near St Mary's Church, and the club returned to its roots 2001. The club song 'Oh When the Saints Go Marching In' is still sung at games. Previously, the Saints were at the compact Dell from 1898, where American troops played several games of American football during the Second World

This 'Long Live Dubcek' graffiti is still just visible over fifty years later.

Ted Bates was a Saints player, manager, director and club president.

War. Other grounds had previously experimented but the Dell was the first professional football ground to have permanent floodlights installed. On 31 October 1950 a friendly game took place against Bournemouth and Boscombe Athletic under these new lights.

Christ Church Freemantle, the Freemantle Arms and the Stile Inn in Shirley Road were all connected with Freemantle FC. In the late 1800s they rivalled Southampton St Mary's (later Southampton FC) as the top local football team. Their black and white kit led to the nickname of the Magpies, and their ground still exists off Shirley Road (later the Civil Service Sports Ground). The Saints eventually overtook them by fully adopting professionalism and joining the Southern League on its foundation in 1894. Freemantle's flirtation with professionalism failed, a proposed merger with the Saints in 1896 floundered and they folded in 1906.

In 1966 England won the World Cup under Alf Ramsey's management. Alf played ninety times as a right back for Southampton FC from 1943–49. Southampton FC legend Terry Paine (b. 1939) was in the 1966 World Cup winning squad managed by Alf, but only played once against Mexico. He finally got a World Cup winners medal in 2009. Winchester-born Terry holds the appearance record for the Saints, having played 713 times, scoring 160 goals between 1957 and 1974.

Did Biggles Live in Southampton?

Air Commodore Arthur Wellesley Bigsworth (1885–1961) lived from around 1901 until 1920 at the former Firgrove House, Moorhill Road, West End. In the First World War he was a lieutenant, commanding No. 1 Squadron, based at Calshot Naval Air Station on Southampton Water. Bigsworth was the first pilot to sink a German U-14 submarine. He also dropped 20-pound bombs at night on a German Zeppelin airship, severely damaging it. While at the Air Ministry he worked with Captain W. E. Johns, who wrote ninety-eight Biggles adventure books from 1932 onwards about the exploits in the First World War of a James Bigglesworth. Confusingly, a 1918 combat report by a pilot with the name of Major James Bigglesworth was recently found at the RAF Museum in a collection of papers that once belonged to Biggles author W. E. Johns.

Southampton and Fish Fingers

Clarence Birdseye test-marketed herring fingers, a product he had discovered in the United States under the name 'herring savouries'. These were tested in Southampton and South Wales against 'cod sticks', a bland product used as a control. Shoppers confounded expectations by showing an overwhelming preference for the cod, and the rest is history. Birds Eye launched their fish fingers in September 1955. The advertising campaign was 'No bones, no waste, no smell, no fuss'.

Southampton's Multicultural Tradition

Like most ports, Southampton has a long multicultural heritage. The merchant Cristoforo Ambruogi, also known as Christopher Ambrose, was from Florence. He became mayor in 1486–87 and in 1497–98. He lived in the medieval parish of All Saints, near the Bargate, and owned a number of ships. He leased the Wool House (today the Dancing Man) at the end of Bugle Street and traded in fine wines, confectionery, fruit, alum and cloth.

In the 1500s we had Walloon and French Protestants settle in the Old Town. The Huguenots were known for their silk-weaving skills, and there is a mulberry tree in the Huguenot garden today in Town Quay Park. St Julien's Church in Winkle Street is known as the 'French Church' and still holds an annual service in French. In 1838, Southampton elected the country's first Jewish councillor, Abraham Abraham, who was a High Street jeweller. He was the sheriff in 1842, but never became mayor. In May 1937 we provided shelter for nearly 4,000 Basque children displaced by the bombing by the Luftwaffe of Guernica in Spain. Black History Month started locally in 2005 and happens every October. A number of plaques have been put around the city including to Bob Marley, who played a gig in the Coach House club at the rear of the Fleming Arms in 1972; and to Mae Street Kidd, Red Cross pioneer, at the Royal South Hants Hospital.

The SS *Shieldhall*

This former River Clyde sewage ship has been run locally since 1988 by volunteers. It departs from Southampton in the summer months and its days out are always highly rated on Tripadvisor. The Shieldhall Song is played on-board and was originally made in support of the Upper Clyde Shipbuilders strike that lasted from 1971–72. The song featured on an album called *Unity Creates Strength* and is credited to the Laggan. The chorus says:

> We're the crew of the SS Shieldhall,
> Pull your chain and we'll answer your call,
> A terrible aroma,
> Will put you in a coma,
> We're the crew of the SS Shieldhall

Woolston Ferry Song

The song, to the tune of the 'Midnight Special', is from 1977 when the ferry was replaced by the Itchen Bridge. It is was written by Mike Sadler and credited to Gutta Percha and the Balladeers, and can be found on YouTube. It sold so well locally that it was number one in the local chart, even outselling Elvis Presley when he died. The ferry service had run from 1836 and one of the old floating bridges is now a restaurant in Bursledon. The initial charge for the bridge was 16 pence, and there is still a toll today.

> If you're ever up in Sholing
> And you want to go to town
> Don't you go by Bitterne
> That's the long way round
> Take a trip across the ferry
> Take a trip across the sea
> And if you're a pedestrian
> You can go for free
> On the Woolston Ferry
> It doesn't travel very fast
> It was never built for comfort
> It was built to last

The initial charge for the Itchen Bridge was 16 pence and there is still a toll today.

The River Test or Anton?

The River Anton was once the preferred name of the River Test. The Anton is first recorded north of Redbridge in Robert Morden's Map of Hampshire in 1720. The first edition of the Ordnance Survey 1 inch to 1 mile map of Southampton and district (1810), gave Anton and Test as equally valid alternatives. Projected, but rejected, ward names for Southampton under the 1837 included Anton ward. Philip Brannon refers to the 'River Test or Anton' in *A Picture of Southampton* in 1850. The name survives today as a small tributary of the River Test flowing through Andover.

Where is Soton?

A visitor might say, 'I've found Woolston, Bitterne, Portswood, Bassett and Shirley but I just can't find Soton.' For locals, Soton, together with the name Sotonian, does not seem unusual. Soton and Sotonian were both used to describe the city and its residents by journalists at the *Daily Echo*, who found Southampton or Southamptonian far too long to fit into the headlines. *Echo* journalist C. F. Carr told local Rotary Club members in 1957, 'These words were produced for convenience in newspaper headlines. The abbreviations for Southampton and Southamptonian were invented by the Southern Daily Echo years ago.' In 1896, King Edward VI Grammar School launched a school magazine, entitled *Sotoniensis*, a Latin name reflecting the academic tradition by which Oxford and Cambridge become Oxoniensis and Cantabrigiensis. Saxon Southampton, which was in the St Mary's area, was originally Hamton or Hamwic. The Saxon name

'Hamwic' for the town first appeared in writing in 721, and the first time Hampton appeared was in 755. A charter of King Edgar of 962 was the first time the name 'Suthampton' appeared in writing. A current Woolston micropub is Olaf's Tun. This was possibly the original name for Woolston when the Vikings had a small fort, or 'tun', here in 994 AD, which they named after their leader Olaf I of Norway – hence, Olaf's Tun. The Domesday Book records the name as 'Olvestune' in 1086 AD and this morphed into 'Woolston' over the years.

'Acha Mush!'

Locals are familiar with the word 'mush' for 'mate' in Southampton. 'Mush' may have derived from the Romany gypsy word for man. The greeting 'acha' instead of 'hi there' probably came from the Hindi word *achcha* for 'okay'. The first Indians came to Southampton in the Victorian times, usually those that worked for the British Army or the East India Company. Other phrases used locally are 'nipper' for a young male and 'dinlo' for anyone you don't have a high regard for. Such local dialect words are heard much less commonly today. Some older residents remember back slang being spoken in the Northam/Chapel area of Southampton. The first letter is moved to the end of a word and 'ay' added on the end – so backslang would become 'ackslangbay'.

The Civic Centre Bomb

On 6 November 1940 George Brown was the town sergeant, taking children and their teachers around the art school at the recently finished Civic Centre when it was bombed. When the air-raid warning sounded he took them into the basement for safety. Sadly bombs hit and he, along with fourteen of the children, perished. In 2006, Paul Tickner, himself a former town sergeant, wrote a booklet chronicling the history of the town sergeants of Southampton over the last 700 years. The book was dedicated to George, as he was the only one to lose his life in the execution of his duties.

DID YOU KNOW?
The Civic Centre was the first building in the country to have the name Civic Centre. It was once a large open space and used by locals for the memorial service following the sinking of *Titanic* in 1912.

DID YOU KNOW?
During medieval times there was the Magdalene Hospital for lepers. Over time, 'Magdalene' became 'Marlands'.

Left: The west entrance to the Civic Centre.

Below: A refuge for lepers was set up in 1172.

5. How Well Do You Know Southampton?

Southampton's Listed Buildings

Southampton has almost 500 listed buildings. They range from the twelfth century Medieval Merchants' House on French Street to the Grade II listed Wyndham Court, the late 1960s-built large block of flats near the Central railway station. After the war damage, many places tried to rebuild them exactly as before. Southampton, however, decided to build a number of blocks in the then modern brutalist style in its post-Second World War reconstruction phase. Built from 1966–1969, Wyndham Court is meant to remind us of the great liners such as the *Queen Elizabeth* and *Queen Mary* that once frequently came to Southampton. The name comes from Sir Charles Wyndham (1638–1706), who was a popular Southampton MP from 1679–98. He gained a reputation for defending tenants against landlords. His coat of arms is one of those above the central arch of the Bargate.

Wyndham Court is a Grade II listed example of brutalism.

Southampton the Spa Town (1760–1820)

In the early 1800s, during Southampton's spa town period, a good public image was needed to attract visitors. Many wealthy people came to sample the Chalybeate Spa waters. Spa Road, at the back of the Above Bar branch of Boots, recalls this period. The

This pump was to dampen down the dust that was being kicked up by horses.

streets were congested with carts and wagons and the Corporation (Now Southampton Council) removed unattended vehicles from the town. They would be taken just north of the walls and impounded by being chained to a tree in what became Poundtree Road. This pump near the cenotaph was to wet the unmade road and dampen down the dust that was being kicked up by horses.

The popularity of Southampton during this period meant a huge increase in horses pulling carts and coaches, and manure in the streets was a problem – hence a boot scraper by the front door! Many boot scrapers still exist in the Bedford Place, Inner Avenue and Oxford Street areas of Southampton. Also during the spa period, the area to the north-east of Arundel Tower (the present-day Waterstones site in Westquay) was a botanical garden. The chalybeate spring there had ferrous waters that were said to cure jaundice, scurvy, yellow fever, barrenness in women, feebleness in young females and rabies. The spa was 15s a year or 2d a glass. The poor could drink free before 8 a.m.

Southampton's Speakers' Corner

Rarely used today, the speakers' corner dates from 1971. It is located in Hoglands Park, opposite Debenhams. It was a direct result of the pedestrianisation of the central Above Bar area, as various individuals and groups had started using the new precinct to promote their cause. This could cause congestion, resulting in the need for a police presence, and some arrests were made. In November 1971 a number of protesters came before the court. They claimed that they were acting within their rights because the Above Bar precinct

Speakers' Corner in Hoglands Park, opposite Debenhams.

was a public space. However, the prosecution argued that the precinct was still technically a highway and not a public space. This still seems to be the case today and is the reason cyclists can go through the precinct without committing an offence. At a council meeting on 10 November 1971, Councillor Alan Reynard proposed a site in Hoglands Park should be used and the following evening the *Southern Daily Echo* announced, 'Southampton has Speakers' Corner'.

The Strawberry Fields of Shirley

Shirley had a thriving market gardening economy until the late 1800s, but the area is all housing today. Shirley and Freemantle joined as suburbs of Southampton in 1895.

Today the area is all housing.

Today the footbridge is across Monks Brook at the Concorde Club.

The Queen Mary Footbridge
This footbridge is to be found across Monks Brooks at the Concorde Club. The *Queen Mary* had its maiden voyage from Southampton in 1936.

Hythe and Hotspur
In 1889, the Percy family took over the running of the ferries across Southampton Water to Hythe. They were descendants of Sir Henry Percy, a late medieval nobleman known as Sir Harry Hotspur and immortalised by William Shakespeare. Many of the ferry boats were named 'Hotspur' In his honour.

The Grace Dieu
Henry V's flagship *The Grace Dieu* was built at the bottom of the High Street in 1420 and designed by William Soper. He was a burgess of Southampton and clerk of the king's ships. At 66 metres long, she was the biggest ship in the world at the time – twice the size of the *Mary Rose* – and needed a specially built dock for her construction near Town Quay. The Hundred Years' War with France was going well for the English after the victory at Agincourt in 1415 and she went on just one voyage, a patrol of the Solent. After being mothballed at Bursledon, she was struck by lightning and burnt to the waterline. The remains can still just be seen today at low tide. In 2005, *Time Team* made a special programme about her.

Changing Stations
The original train station at Blechynden stood further east than the present-day Central station, stretching nearly to the entrance of the tunnel. It was built soon after the opening of the Southampton–Dorchester line in 1847. That line was known as 'Castleman's Corkscrew' after its designer, and the non-direct route it was forced to take to accommodate the interests of some landowners. The station name was changed to Southampton West in 1858 and then to Southampton Central in 1935.

Spinal Tap
The Guitar Store is in Wyndham Court, near Southampton Central station. It has a nod to the cult *Spinal Tap* film (1984) as the master volume control goes to 11.

The volume control goes up to eleven.

Neville Shute (1889–1960)

The April 1939 book *What Happened to the Corbetts* by Shute is a fictional account of the effect of aerial bombing on Southampton. A thousand copies were distributed free to members of the Air Raid Precautions team to inform them of what to expect. By the autumn of 1940 fiction had turned into reality.

The American Wall

Hidden in plain sight on Western Esplanade by the Grand Harbour Hotel, this remaining bit of wall is a direct link to the US servicemen who gathered in Southampton before and after D-Day in June 1944. Many carved their names and home state on the wall. Southampton became the US Army's fourteenth major port in preparation for the invasion of northern France. When Southampton councillor Reginald Stranger was mayor in 1944 he greeted the millionth American GI – Sergeant Shimer from Chambersburg, Pennsylvania – to pass through the port en route to the Normandy Beaches. The mayor promised to provide for the soldier's daughter should anything happen to him. Unfortunately he was killed in April 1945. Councillor Stranger established a trust fund for this daughter. As a 'thank you', 600 bushels (19,000 pounds in weight) of apples were sent as a gift to Southampton children from his home town. 'Every apple which is being distributed comes to you with the love and affection of the people of Chambersburg,' Councillor Stranger told the youngsters of Bassett Green School as he gave away the fruit. On 16 January 1945 the 2 millionth American soldier passed through Southampton. By the end of the war in Europe, in May 1945, around 3.5 million Allied military personnel had passed through. Locals said the Yanks were 'over paid, over sexed and over here!'

Many US troops carved their names and home state on the wall.

Above: By May 1945 around 3.5 million Allied military personnel had passed through Southampton.

Left: Locals said the Yanks were 'over paid, over sexed and over here!'

Second World War Plane Crash

The only German plane to crash in Southampton was a Heinkel bomber in Padwell Road on the night of 15/16 April 1941. Charles Wyatt House, an Age Concern Day Care centre, now occupies the Innere Avenue site. The crew bailed out; two were killed when their parachutes failed to open, one injured his leg and another was unhurt.

A One-handed Clock

The fifteenth-century St Nicholas' Church, North Stoneham, has a clock with only an hour hand. It is thought the workers in the surrounding fields did not need to know about minutes, just the hour.

Going Dotty

James Dott, a retired East India Company surgeon, lived at the Grade II listed Bitterne Grove from 1791–1843. It is now St Mary's Independent School. The lower part of Midanbury Lane was known as Dott's Lane into the twentieth century. Some say that the word 'dotty', meaning a confused or eccentric person, stems from his unusual behaviour.

It is thought the workers in the surrounding fields did not need to know about minutes, just the hour.

Falkland War Memorials

There is a plaque in Holy Rood and another small and rather tucked away one in Mayflower Park. Older locals will remember ships such as the *Canberra* being prepared in Southampton with a specially fitted flight deck. Many went to see the homecoming of the *QE2* to her home port on 11 June 1982 after her 14,000-mile journey. She had served as a troopship and helicopter carrier. It then took nine weeks of work to convert her back to a luxury liner.

QE2 Anchor

This is outside the ruins of Holyrood Church. The maiden voyage of the *QE2* was from Southampton in May 1969. She left Southampton for the last time in November 2008 and headed for Port Rashid in Dubai. In 2018 she was converted to a restaurant and hotel.

QE2's anchor, just outside Holy Rood.

A Roman road ran through Bitterne to Chichester.

Roman Southampton – Clausentum

Marcus Aurelius Carausius lived in the small trading post of Clausentum, the present-day Bitterne Manor area, on the bend of the River Itchen. He was admiral of the Channel and North Sea fleet who rebelled in 286 AD and set himself up as independent ruler of Roman Britain. Local coins have been found with his image. He was assassinated after seven years.

Standing in the Dock at Southampton

Southampton has been mentioned twice in No. 1 hit songs. 'The Ballad of John and Yoko' by the Beatles (released in 1969) tells of their unsuccessful attempt to get to 'Holland or France' from the dock at Southampton. They had turned up without a booking or passports. The 'man in the mac' was Bill Le Poidevin, who was very surprised when he was told he was in a song. In 2010, Tinie Tempah mentioned Southampton in 'Pass Out'. Pink Floyd also had a Southampton Dock song on their 1983 album *The Final Cut*. In 1997, the *Titanic* film featured a tune called 'Southampton' on its soundtrack.

The Last Night of the Proms often features 'Poor Tom Bowling', which was written by Charles Dibdin (1745–1814), who was baptised at Holyrood Church. 'The Bells of St Mary's' was sung by Bing Crosby in the 1940 film of the same name. It was originally written after a visit to Southampton back in 1914 by two songwriters who had heard the then new bells of our own St Mary's Church. American Douglas Furber and his co-writer, the Australian A. Emmett Adams, wrote 'The Bells of St Mary's' following a visit. The song is also on the 1963 *A Christmas Gift for You from Phil Spector*, sung by Bob B. Soxx and the Blue Jeans.

All That Jazz

The famous jazz trumpeter Louis Armstrong played at the former Hippodrome Theatre in Ogle Road in 1932. He also sat in with a local band led by Southampton violinist and sax player Gill Hume, who was a well-known local dance band leader from the 1930s to the 1960s. More recently, jazz saxophonist Courtney Pine received an honorary doctorate from the University of Southampton in 2010. When the liner *France* docked at Southampton on 5 October 1967, singer Mama Cass Elliot (1941–74) was arrested by Scotland Yard Special Branch officers and held at Southampton Police Station, then in the Civic Centre. The arrest was to do with an unpaid hotel bill from a previous visit; however, it is thought the police were really interested in a male companion called Pic Dawson, who was allegedly involved with importing drugs into the UK. She was released but a Mamas and Papas concert was cancelled at the Royal Albert Hall.

Remember You're a Sotonian

Born in Southampton in 1949, Mike Batt has been a singer-songwriter, musician, record producer and conductor. He is best known for creating the Wombles, writing the chart-topping song 'Bright Eyes' and discovering Katie Melua. Chris Packham, the naturalist and TV presenter was born in Southampton in 1961. Southampton's Ken Russell (1927–2011), the film director, once lived in Belmont Road, Portswood, but there is no blue plaque there. Radio 1 presenter Scott Mills was born in nearby Eastleigh in 1974 and was awarded an honorary doctorate of Arts from Southampton Solent University in 2009. The bridge that crosses the M3 at Fleet Services was officially named the Scott Mills Bridge in March 2016. Female impersonator Danny La Rue (1927–2009) was an adopted Sotonian, living here for twenty-one years, lastly near the Bitterne Park side of Cobden Bridge.

Film and TV

Some of Jonathan Miller's TV play *Alice in Wonderland* was shot at the Netley Military Hospital just before it was demolished in 1966. Also in 1966, the Oscar-winning film *A Man For All Seasons* was filmed at the Beaulieu River (standing in for the Thames). From 1979–1981 *Worzel Gummidge* was filmed around Romsey. In the 1980s, Sam Costa was a manager at the Joiners Arms music venue. He had previously been a stunt double for Roger Moore (1927–2017) in James Bond films. In 1991 Fritham featured in the Kevin Costner movie *Robin Hood: Prince of Thieves*. In 2014, Southampton Docks were used in TV spin-off show *24: Live Another Day*, with Kiefer Sutherland playing Jack Bauer.

Lowry and the Floating Bridge

Artist L. S. Lowry (1887–1976) often visited Southampton. In 1956 he painted two pictures of the Floating Bridge, which was replaced in 1977 by the Itchen Bridge. One is owned by the City Art Gallery; the other sold for £220,000 in 1999. There is a commonly held belief that the council at the time said that Itchen Bridge tolls would cease when its building costs were paid. True or not, tolls remain in place over forty years on.

Lest We Forget

Southampton Cenotaph has 2,008 names of those who fell in the First World War. It was unveiled in November 1920 and was designed by Sir Edwin Lutyens (1869–1944), who also designed the Cenotaph in Whitehall, London. A bench in Hollybrook Cemetery by David Banks is a memorial to the civilians who were killed by enemy action in Southampton during the Second World War. The back of the bench is made from the rubble of buildings destroyed when the town was targeted during the Blitz in 1940. The cemetery also contains the Hollybrook Memorial, which is the nation's memorial to the 1,852 officers and men from land or air forces who have no grave. It was built by the War Graves Commission and was the last First World War memorial to be built in 1930. Southampton had been the primary embarkation point and was the last bit of English soil some stood on before leaving on a troop ship. The youngest person was seventeen and the oldest – at sixty-five – was Secretary of State for War, Field Marshal Kitchener (1850–1916), who died when HMS *Hampshire* was struck by a German mine.

Above left: The cenotaph was designed by Sir Edwin Lutyens.

Above right: The Hollybrook Memorial was built by the War Graves Commission in 1930 and was the last National First World War memorial.

David Cameron

The former prime minister's great-great-great-great-grandparents lived at Bevois Mount House, off Lodge Road from 1808–40. They were Henry and Sophia Hulton, who married in Millbrook. When Cameron appeared on *Desert Island Discs* he said 'Ernie' (1971) by Southampton's Benny Hill was his favourite song and he could recite it in full.

The original 1846 Royal Southern Yacht Club premises at No. 1 Bugle Street.

The Cross House provided shelter for passengers on the old Itchen Ferry boats.

The Cross House was mentioned in 1577, but it was probably constructed earlier in the medieval period.

The K6 art gallery uses these twin 1930s former phone boxes for exhibitions.

Clock Tower as seen through the *Enclosure* sculpture from 2000. It acts as a picture frame for local landmarks.

Above: South Western House was built as a hotel around 1865. Churchill and Eisenhower are said to have met there. Today it is seventy-seven apartments.

Right: This Bitterne Park Triangle Clock Tower was situated in Above Bar Street and New Road until 1935.

About the Author

I am a born and bred Sotonian and love the pursuit of trivial information. After a career in further and higher education, I became a qualified tour guide and a founder member of See Southampton. I have also played keyboards in local bands for many years and have a keen interest in all forms of music and the history of local entertainment. Being taken by my dad to the Dell Football Ground as a boy has led to a lifetime of supporting Southampton Football Club. In 2017, I had a long hospital stay following a brain haemorrhage and writing this book has been a new challenge I have enjoyed immensely – proof indeed that, as the eighteenth-century occasional Southampton resident poet Alexander Pope said, 'hope springs eternal in the human breast'.

The author, Martin Brisland.

Acknowledgements

My name may be on the cover, but this book has been a team effort. Sincere thanks are due to Jenny and Carolann for all their support and to my son Alexander for his photography and Carolina for her technical help. My tour guide colleagues in See Southampton are a fountain of local knowledge. Godfrey, Steve and myself have jointly run our successful Facebook page and I owe a great deal to their excellent knowledge and research skills.